La Rochefoucauld

Maximes et Réflexions diverses

Derek A. Watts

Reader in Classical French Literature
University of Exeter

UNIVERSITY OF GLASGOW
FRENCH AND GERMAN PUBLICATIONS
1993

University of Glasgow French and German Publications

Series Editors: Mark G. Ward (German)
Geoff Woollen (French)

Consultant Editors : Colin Smethurst
Kenneth Varty

Modern Languages Building, University of Glasgow,
Glasgow G12 8QL, Scotland.

First published 1993.

Printed by BPCC Wheatons Ltd., Exeter.

ISBN 0 85261 394 6

Contents

Preface

Reference by numbers to the *Maximes* of La Rochefoucauld is complicated by the fact that those not included in the 'definitive' edition of 1678 are differently described and numbered in the currently available editions (see Bibliography, p. 89). The 504 maxims constituting the 1678 edition present no problem, but the remaining ones are either numbered consecutively 505-641, as in editions 1, 2, and 3 of our bibliography; or they are separately listed in editions 4, 5, 6, and 7 as 'maximes supprimées' if they were included in at least one early edition and subsequently eliminated, or as 'maximes posthumes / écartées / non publiées' if they did not appear in print in the author's lifetime. There are sound scholarly reasons for this attempt to distinguish the 'apocrypha' from the 'canon', but it has produced so many discrepancies in numbering between the available editions that the older numbering (1-641) has been preferred for all references to be given in the present study. However, all the current editions which adopt a different scheme include a table of concordance which should enable the reader to trace easily the maxims referred to here as nos. 505-641.

Page references to the *Réflexions diverses* are to the Nouveaux Classiques Larousse edition (*1* of the Bibliography). The italicized figures in parentheses refer to the numbers in this bibliography; ordinary figures in parentheses refer to the individual maxims.

Introduction

Not many works of literature have produced such an impact, despite their modest dimensions, as the *Maximes* of La Rochefoucauld. Their author soon achieved fame as the principal inventor and unrivalled practitioner of the maxim, that most quotable of literary forms. For Voltaire, in 1751, the *Maximes* were no less than 'un des ouvrages qui contribuèrent le plus à former le goût de la nation, et à lui donner un esprit de justesse et de précision'. Nor was this writer's fame confined to the French-speaking world: the first English translation of the *Maximes* had appeared as early as 1670. In 1823, William Hazlitt published, anonymously, his *Characteristics: in the manner of Rochefoucault's Maxims*. Such a title was in itself a sufficient advertisement in nineteenth-century London. In 1958, the *New Statesman* offered one of its weekly literary prizes for a 'set of four maxims from a La Rochefoucauld *de nos jours*'. The epigrammatic pungency of the form inevitably enhanced the impression of cynicism produced by the central theme, that of man's incurable egoism or *amour-propre*. If one knew anything about La Rochefoucauld, it was that he came to bury humanity and not to praise it. The *Maximes* have been described as 'l'épitaphe de la féodalité mourante', as the autopsy of their author's generation of turbulent aristocrats, soon to be tamed and confined to the antechambers of Versailles. However, many of these brief texts, deceptively limpid on a rapid reading, are rich in ambiguity; they have a knack of yielding unexpected interpretations when looked at afresh. La Rochefoucauld combines, in a most fascinating manner, three contradictory currents which were central to French Classicism: aristocratic idealism, grim Jansenist austerity, and the fashionable culture of the salons. I shall try to put his work in its historical context in order to clarify its message, or its diverse messages; but the very nature of the maxim is to resist such attempts at categorisation. Its unique power lies not so much in instruction as in provocation, in stimulating each reader to produce an appreciative or angry response. Moreover, this seemingly impersonal and abstract prose not only embodies a passionate quest for the self, but is by no means devoid of artistic vision.

Chapter One

Background

Such an elusive writer invites misinterpretations of all kinds. The best way to reduce this risk is to place him as firmly as possible, though of necessity rather briefly, in the context of his own time.

The career and intellectual development of La Rochefoucauld are vividly illustrative of the changing perspectives of seventeenth-century French society, and in particular of the groups to which he belonged: the aristocracy, and what we may perhaps already call the intelligentsia. Born in 1613, he lived his youth and early manhood under the iron rule of Cardinal Richelieu, whose power lasted from 1624 to 1642. Despite intense political strife, these years can be seen as part of a predominately optimistic age, in which various intellectual and religious movements combined to produce an atmosphere of 'confidence in man'. The prevailing influence in the religious sphere was that of 'l'humanisme dévot', a product of the Catholic Counter-Reformation, consisting essentially of two beliefs: the vital importance of human choice and effort, aided by sovereign free will, in achieving Christian salvation; and the compatibility of life in elegant society and of moderate indulgence in its pleasures, with that same perspective of redemption. The writings of Saint François de Sales, and in particular his *Introduction à la vie dévote* (1608-1609), are richly illustrative of this optimism. The aristocratic aspect of this confidence is visible in a popular literary genre of the time, namely the panegyric of the Hero. Any military victory would immediately give rise to eulogies in prose and verse, lauding the triumphant general almost as a demi-god. Their equivalent in the contemporary theatre is found in Corneille's epic narrative of Rodrigue's victory over the Moors in *Le Cid* (1637). The best-known works of this dramatist propose a code of heroic conduct, often known as 'l'éthique de la gloire', in which is idealised the instinctive pride of the *grand seigneur*. Heroic aspirations were manifest in the realm of love as well as in war. The most successful novel of the century, *L'Astrée* by Honoré d'Urfé—a vast *roman-fleuve* (1607-1627) for which La Rochefoucauld had a lifelong attachment—portrays love above all as an ardent submission to the lady's 'divine' perfections, reminiscent both of medieval chivalry and of the neo-Platonism which had flourished in the previous century. In the sphere of moral philosophy, however, the most influential doctrine was a Christianised form of stoicism, according to which virtue lies in the disposition of the will to follow reason and to overcome passion, which is described, in the Stoic tradition, as 'false opinion' (*40*, pp. 73-95). The supreme virtue is therefore *la constance*, noble fortitude, but this is not a wholly passive attitude: it includes courageous enterprise and civic zeal. The neo-Stoic ethic implies a sanguine view of man's capacity to direct his own fate. Much the same implication is to be found in the final landmark in the history of 'optimistic' ethical doctrines in seventeenth-century France, namely Descartes's *Traité des passions de l'âme* (1649).

The middle years of the century, however, mark a watershed. Politically, they were dominated by a civil war known as the Fronde, which raged intermittently between 1649 and 1653. Richelieu's authoritarian policies, accompanied by heavy taxation, were much less successfully pursued from 1643 by his successor Mazarin. The overthrow of this 'usurper' was the prime objective of the highly unstable coalitions of rebels—noblemen and *parlementaires*—which formed and fell apart during this period of intense civil strife. Their defeat in 1652-1653 marked the end, in public opinion, of the aristocracy's claim to embody any ideals of *gloire, générosité* or *constance*. Many of the countless propaganda pamphlets (*mazarinades*) printed during the Fronde denounced the ravages of *l'intérêt*, naked self-interest, accompanied as it was by the utmost treachery and a good deal of violence. Mazarin survived at the helm of State for another eight years after the Fronde, and he saw to it that the young King was well schooled in the lessons of recent French history. From the moment Louis XIV embarked on his 'personal reign' in 1661, the overriding objective of his domestic policies was to ensure that another Fronde would never occur. The systematic 'domestication' of the nobility, henceforth consigned to the Court, the army, or to oblivion, was to be a prime instrument of that objective. Among its effects were bitter disillusionment and enforced idleness.

The dynamism so apparent among the French nobility during the early part of the century was thus gradually eroded by this and other factors, including, in many cases, increasing financial difficulties. The same years saw the rise of a religious movement, Jansenism, that was to claim an impressive number of converts among both the aristocracy and the class of *officiers royaux* that had most suffered from political change and civil war. Cornelius Jansen, bishop of Ypres, had written the seminal work, a learned and reverent commentary in Latin on the theology of St Augustine, appropriately entitled the *Augustinus* (1640). Jansenist doctrine and moral attitudes somewhat resembled those of the Puritans in contemporary England. Of all the Holy Fathers, it was Augustine who had most insisted on the irremediable corruption of human nature resulting from the Fall, and on the impossibility of salvation without the aid of a Divine Grace both compelling and arbitrary, that is, not granted in response to any merit or entreaty. Far from seeing will and reason as the most vital characteristics of mankind, the Jansenist writers, and foremost among them Pascal, tended to describe human nature as a battleground of conflicting interests, impulses and passions. Even the most Christian-seeming deeds or thoughts were not to be accounted virtuous, in the Jansenist view, unless they were prompted not by *amour-propre* in its various disguises, but by true charity inspired by Divine Grace. This was the French version of a controversy that has been described as 'le débat exemplaire qui divisa l'Europe occidentale pendant plus d'un siècle' (*52*, p. 553), between neo-Stoic confidence in human nature and Jansenist (or Puritan) distrust of its frailty. Among the questions the Jansenists asked most insistently were: 'Is 'natural' virtue—that is, virtue not dependent on Divine Grace—of any worth from a Christian point of view?' and 'Are the pleasures of refined social life compatible with salvation?'. Their answers were firmly in the negative.

Not every Jansenist, however, was as rigorous a convert as Pascal. Many of their *sympathisants* continued to compromise with the world, to frequent the salons and cultivate the social graces. Among Mme de Sablé's circle of friends, frequented by La Rochefoucauld, we shall find doctrinally intransigent Jansenists like Jacques Esprit, who was never a recluse despite his uncompromising theology. Moreover in some of the salons that opened their doors after the Fronde there was earnest discussion of weighty moral questions rather than the frivolities lampooned by Molière. None of the wide-ranging subject-matter broached in the *Maximes et Réflexions,* from the nature of heroism to the antics of amorous dotards, from the problem of pagan virtue to the self-indulgence involved in mourning a loved one, could be considered beyond the ken, or the curiosity, of an audience such as La Rochefoucauld addressed.

The Author

François VI de La Rochefoucauld (1613-1680) was by birth the most illustrious writer of his age. His family tree reached back to the eleventh century. The dukedom, however, was of more recent vintage, having been conferred in 1622 on his father for distinguished army service. Our author's early education seems to have been neglected: the young François learned little Latin, but eagerly devoured fashionable romances such as *Amadis de Gaule* and *L'Astrée.* From such reading he no doubt derived his youthful thirst for extraordinary, heroic exploits, as indeed he confesses in his *Mémoires (2,* p. 50). A young *seigneur* had to grow up fast in those times: the Prince de Marcillac (as our author was known until his father's death in 1650) was married at fourteen, and embarked on his first military campaign little more than a year later. He soon turned to court intrigue as a more reliable means of personal advancement. Touched by the sad beauty of Louis XIII's neglected Queen, Anne of Austria, he inevitably found himself plotting against her persecutor, Richelieu. This involved collaboration with one of the great political schemers among the *grandes dames* of the time, Mme de Chevreuse, the first of four females whose successive influence, according to Sainte-Beuve and other biographers, dominated the life of our author. (The others were Mme de Longueville, Mme de Sablé and Mme de La Fayette.) A plot was hatched in which Marcillac was to abduct Anne of Austria to join the exiled Queen Mother, Marie de Médicis, in Brussels. However, a false alarm caused Mme de Chevreuse to flee the country prematurely, with the aid of horses borrowed from Marcillac, though without his permission. Richelieu promptly ordered his arrest and incarceration in the Bastille, though for only one week, after which he was exiled to his estates at Verteuil near Angoulême. There Marcillac subsequently spent most of his time, when not on military service, until the death of Richelieu in 1642. He had become a martyr in his own eyes, and the stage was thus set for his role in the Fronde.

There were, however, two more immediate and potent causes for his rebellious activities during the civil war. The first was the *affaire des tabourets* in 1649. The *tabouret* in question was a stool on which princesses of the Blood and duchesses of ancient lineage were allowed to sit in the Queen's presence. To acquire this privilege was the great current ambition of the house of La Rochefoucauld, and Marcillac pursued it with a frenzy that demonstrates how vital were such matters of privilege and precedence among the court aristocracy at that time. The *tabouret* was several times promised by Mazarin to the duchesse de La Rochefoucauld, as she was now called—the recently inherited title greatly increased the justice of her cause, at first very dubious—but the undertaking was never honoured, and the young Duke's fury knew no bounds. The other influence which led him to play such an active part in the Fronde was the greatest amorous attachment of his life, one which like so many such liaisons had political as well as amorous dimensions. About 1646, he had become the lover of Mme de Longueville, sister to the Prince de Condé, who was soon to become the leading rebel of the second Fronde. A woman of dazzling beauty, she was passionately ambitious for her house, with the result that biographers and historians have been arguing ever since as to which of the couple was the exploiter and which the victim. The honours were no doubt equally shared; but La Rochefoucauld's role in all this was already marked by the hesitancy and the detachment that so often characterised his conduct. Nevertheless, when Mme de Longueville deserted him in 1652, he felt a profound rage and bitterness that must have left their mark on his personality. Soon after this setback, he was grievously wounded at a decisive combat in front of the ramparts of Paris, near the Porte Saint-Antoine, where Condé's dwindling forces were fortunate to escape annihilation. Threatened with the loss of his sight, and utterly disillusioned, La Rochefoucauld withdrew to his estates, and though he proudly refused the first amnesty offered him, he eventually made his peace with the Court. He was granted another army commission, but he never regained the King's favour; in 1671, he even made over the ducal title to his eldest son, now an ambitious courtier in his own right.

It may be presumed that during these years of tedious exile, La Rochefoucauld sought to repair his defective education by extensive reading, applying himself to the philosophers and historians of antiquity, such as Epicurus, Seneca and Tacitus. At least the *Maximes* suggest some acquaintance with these sources, as with certain French writers, foremost among them Montaigne. He also set to work on his *Mémoires,* a work which on its own merits would have earned him a modest reputation.

He was permitted to return to Paris in 1656, and took up residence in the Hôtel de Liancourt, in the rue de Seine, near the Luxembourg. It was the property of his uncle, the Duke of that name, one of the earliest and most fervent devotees of the Jansenist cause. Other prominent Jansenists were regular visitors there— Jacques Esprit, for instance—and in this atmosphere of civilised but austere piety, La Rochefoucauld settled down to a life of somewhat melancholy retirement, devoted to a limited number of friends and the surviving members of his family. One group of acquaintances was centred on Mme de Sablé's residence nearby. Another was a circle of friends sometimes known as *la société du Luxembourg,* whose fortunes Mme de Sévigné traces in many of her letters. They included Mme de La Fayette, to whom La Rochefoucauld became closely attached, probably about 1664. There are many testimonies to their deep mutual sympathy. She no doubt helped him to maintain a certain serenity despite physical pain due mainly to gout, and the many sorrows that afflicted his old age. In 1672, for instance, at the celebrated crossing of the Rhine by the French army invading Holland, two of his sons were killed—two, that is, if we include the comte de Saint-Paul, the presumed son born of his liaison with Mme de Longueville. She herself was now leading a life of penitent 'retraite' among the Jansenists of Port-Royal. After a long illness aggravated by his war wounds and chronic gout, La Rochefoucauld died in March 1680, aged sixty-six. He appears to have endured a

bleak and melancholy mature age. Were the *Maximes* a direct
expression of bitter personal disillusionment? Maybe so; but in
making this assumption we must avoid the kind of over-
simplification that begs or ignores several inportant questions. We
should beware, for instance, of reading too much into the *Portrait de
Monsieur de La Rochefoucauld par lui-même*, which is often printed
alongside the *Maximes* (e.g. *4,* pp. 251-8; *5,* pp. 221-6; *6,* pp. 265-
70). The quality he depicts most prominently in himself is
'melancholy'. This was regarded at the time as the most dangerous of
the four humours, producing in its acutest form what we would now
call nervous depression. However, La Rochefoucauld does not intend
to be taken quite as literally as this: he is just portraying himself as a
highly sombre and sensitive soul. There is, after all, something quite
distinguished about 'melancholy', as the Romantics later discovered.
Moreover this self-portrait has to be read in the light of its original
context and purpose. It first appeared in 1659 in a celebrated
'gallery' of literary portraits dedicated to Mlle de Montpensier. The
jeu de portraits was then a popular pastime in some of the salons.
Such set pieces, like those which adorned the novels of Mlle de
Scudéry, involved a good deal of flattery; the rules and conventions
of the genre prescribed a certain idealisation of the subject, whether
this was oneself or another person. Accordingly La Rochefoucauld
gives the impression of a man of delicate sensitivity, though apt to
repress all outward show of emotion, and possessed of a great
scrupulousness resulting in all manner of hesitations. At the onset,
for instance, we find him ruminating most curiously over the shape
of his own nose: 'Je serais fort empêché à dire de quelle sorte j'ai le
nez fait, car il n'est ni camus ni aquilin, ni gros ni pointu, au moins à
ce que je crois'. A paltry detail perhaps, but symptomatic of the
hesitancy, the ambiguity that many of La Rochefoucauld's
contemporaries remarked on, for they could never quite make him
out. He acquired the nickname of 'La Franchise', because he boasted
so much of his own candour, but the title quickly became ironical—a
symbol of his alleged deviousness. In an equally famous portrait of
our author by a bitter enemy of yore, Cardinal de Retz, this
indefinability is given its aptest expression in the language of French
classicism: 'Il y a toujours eu du *je ne sais quoi* en tout M. de La
Rochefoucauld'. The overall impression given by this hostile portrait
is of impenetrability and lack of self-knowledge, and of resulting
non-achievement in his public career. No doubt is raised, however,
about the keenness of his intelligence. An influential modern critic,
Starobinski, describes our author's defect quite aptly as 'son manque
d'adhésion à lui-même' (*54,* p. 37). A book of maxims, in its
fragmentary nature and in its successive editions, forms an ideal
medium for entertaining all manner of second thoughts, for adding a

nuance here and a proviso there to what was written last month or last year, for producing yet further refinements to a cumulative portrait of the complexity of man.

Another striking feature of La Rochefoucauld's self-portrait is the persistent vein of stoicism that runs through it. This is curious above all because certain key texts in the *Maximes* deliver, as we shall see, a fierce onslaught on the Stoic philosophers and their ideal of human self-sufficiency. In this 1659 text, however, La Rochefoucauld willingly depicts himself in Stoic colours: 'J'ai toutes les passions assez douces et assez réglées: on ne m'a presque jamais vu en colère. [...] L'ambition ne me travaille point. [...] Je crains peu de choses, et ne crains aucunement la mort.' *Ne me travaille plus* would have been nearer the mark! The last remark may not fully imply that *mépris de la mort* that La Rochefoucauld so eloquently denounces in the grand finale to the successive editions of his *Maximes* (now no. 504)—but it must surely surprise us, particularly since the author adds at once: 'Je suis peu sensible à la pitié, et je voudrais ne l'y être point du tout.' It must however be emphasised that this was a self-portrait for 'public consumption', written according to fixed conventions, in a fixed order of topics first established by Montaigne. Here La Rochefoucauld is portraying himself also as an exemplary *honnête homme*. Such a set exercise does not imply total sincerity, or a once-for-all commitment. When La Rochefoucauld wrote his own portrait of Retz, he characteristically added an alternative version, probably for Mme de Sévigné's eyes, which is rather more benign in its judgements.

Other Writings

Before we turn exclusively to the *Maximes et Réflexions,* two other texts by La Rochefoucauld merit our brief attention. The first is a virulent pamphlet, entitled *Apologie de M. le Prince de Marcillac,* composed at the end of 1648, though not discovered and published for another two centuries. It forms a furious protest at the 'perfidy' of Anne of Austria and Mazarin, centred on the *affaire du tabouret* and accompanied, as the title indicates, by a lengthy self-justification. It is hard to say which is the more striking feature of this text: the arrogance of Marcillac's evocation of his family's prestige—'il n'y a point de souverains dans la chrétienté qui ne soient sortis d'une fille de ma maison'—or the vehement irony of a man deeply wounded in his honour (as he sees it) and, we might add, in his *amour-propre.* From the very onset, every word is a rapier-thrust. Written some seven years before Pascal's *Lettres provinciales,* the *Apologie* is widely regarded today as the earliest landmark of French classical prose at its most accomplished.

La Rochefoucauld's *Mémoires* are just as well written as the *Apologie,* though in a more sober vein. The story of their composition and publication is very complicated, and we cannot follow it in any detail. Suffice it to say that part of the text appeared in a pirate edition, which caused the author acute embarrassment, as early as 1662; yet it was not until 1874 that a completely satisfactory text was established and published. The intentions behind the writing of this work were complicated, too: La Rochefoucauld seeks to explain the reasons for his personal failure, and for that of the entire Fronde, which he now condemns. At other moments, we see him at pains to justify his conduct; or perhaps he simply aims to vie with the historians whose work he so much admired (see *34,* pp. 711-13). The prevailing terseness of the style suggests that his preferred models were Sallust and Tacitus. Sometimes he evokes with nostalgia the heady, *romanesque* adventurism of his youth, sometimes he writes with cold psychological precision. He will not admit to having experienced any passionate feelings for Mme de Longueville, but rather cynically presents his motives concerning her as entirely political. Above all, in the later pages, he gives bitter expression to the disillusionment caused by an ill-starred destiny (*37,* pp. 135-6).

To what extent does the content of the *Mémoires* anticipate that of the *Maximes*? Although the composition of these two works must have overlapped slightly, there are few phrases or sentences which from the formal point of view clearly anticipate the later work; but there are a dozen or so 'pre-maxims', as they might be called, that is, comments on events or individuals that needed only minor reconstruction in order to find a place in La Rochefoucauld's masterwork. On the first page of the *Mémoires* (*2,* p. 39), we learn that Louis XIII 'avait un esprit de détail appliqué uniquement à de petites choses', which foreshadows maxim 41 ('Ceux qui s'appliquent trop aux petites choses deviennent ordinairement incapables des grandes'; cf. no. 569). On the same initial page, we are informed of the strained relations between the royal couple: 'La passion qu'il avait eue depuis longtemps pour la Reine s'était convertie en dépit', which needs a more substantial rewording in order to produce maxim 111: 'Plus on aime une maîtresse, plus on est prêt de la haïr' (cf. *Réflexion* VIII, *1,* p. 123). Buckingham's conduct towards Anne of Austria is described as 'un emportement que l'amour seul peut rendre excusable' (*2,* p. 42); likewise, according to maxim 546, 'la prudence et l'amour ne sont pas faits l'un pour l'autre: à mesure que l'amour croît, la prudence diminue' (cf. no. 638). Narrating a complex amorous intrigue, La Rochefoucauld refers to 'le caprice, qui dispose toujours de la fidélité des amants', a remark which recalls several maxims (334, 484, 577, among others, though none of the parallels is really close). Beaufort, we are told, 'se servait utilement de cette distinction et de ses autres avantages pour établir la faveur, par l'opinion qu'il affectait de donner qu'elle était déjà tout établie' (p. 63), which is quite close to maxim 56: 'Pour s'établir dans le monde, on fait tout ce que l'on peut pour y paraître établi.' Part of La Rochefoucauld's later narrative (pp. 68-9) is a vivid illustration of maxim 378: 'On donne des conseils, mais on n'inspire pas de conduite'. (However, Mme de La Fayette later claimed to be the author of this.) Mazarin's dissimulation, as described on pp. 94-5, is analogous to maxim 117, which begins: 'La plus subtile de toutes les finesses est de savoir bien feindre de tomber dans les pièges que l'on nous tend'. Some remarks on Fortune and on grasping the decisive moment (pp. 97, 122-3, 132) recall several maxims, and notably nos. 45, 343, and 453. But the maxims concerned are not on the whole particularly memorable ones, so perhaps we should beware of exaggerating the importance of this phenomenon. As Starobinski puts it, 'dans la maxime, l'événement vécu cherche et trouve l'oubli' (*54*, p. 36; cf. J. Lafond in *30*, pp. 137-40).

The *Maximes*

The genesis and publication of the *Maximes* raise questions at least as complicated as those involving La Rochefoucauld's *Mémoires*. A legend current for over a century concerned the role of an institution known as 'le salon de Mme de Sablé'. The *Maximes*, it was believed, were the collective product of this assembly, the result of an extended party game—the *jeu de maximes*—in which each of the participants was required to submit a pithy formula on a topic such as love, jealousy, courage, gratitude etc., that had been 'mis sur le tapis'. According to this legend, first concocted in the 1820s by Victor Cousin, La Rochefoucauld was merely the 'secretary' who recorded the maxims as they were spontaneously generated, so to speak, in Mme de Sablé's assemblies, rather than the creator who shaped them in the sweat of his own brow. This myth has now been discredited (see e.g. *24*, or *37*, pp. 201-216). It is not even certain that 'le salon de Mme de Sablé' really existed as a regular institution during the years (1658-1664) when the bulk of the maxims must have seen the light of day. The documents concerned comprise a quantity of correspondence which reveals that the earliest maxims to be composed in this *milieu* were indeed the result of close collaboration or at least consultation, but between only three persons: La Rochefoucauld, Mme de Sablé and Jacques Esprit. Mme de Sablé, a widow who had long been a leading light in *précieux* society, now converted to Jansenist piety but not a complete recluse, had taken up residence in 1656 within the walls of the monastery of Port-Royal de Paris. Her many friends and acquaintances included leading Jansenists, Pascal among them, but also men of learning from many horizons—she was keenly interested in theology, philosophy, psychology, physics and medicine, among other things. Mme de Sablé certainly entertained many visitors—her table was reputed— but she was also an acute hypochondriac, given to barring her door without warning to all comers, for fear of 'le mauvais air'. It is this habit in particular that makes us question whether she organised assemblies numerous or regular enough to merit the title of 'salon'. However, the many documents collected by her physician, a certain Vallant—now known collectively as the 'Portefeuilles Vallant' (see *26*, pp. 89 ff.)—prove abundantly that her circle of acquaintances included not only persons notable for their social graces, but also experts in various fields of learning. As for Jacques Esprit, he was a theologian by training, having twice studied at the Oratoire, where his brother Thomas was a resident priest; but his literary activities had earned him membership of the Académie Française at the age of only thirty-nine. He had been the *intendant* of La Rochefoucauld's household from 1652 to 1657 or thereabouts; their friendship had probably begun several years earlier. In 1678, he published a treatise of great moral severity, entitled *La Fausseté des vertus humaines.* It treats the dominating theme of the *Maximes,* the one announced in its title, in the form of a learned and ponderous dissertation, emphasizing the Christian solution to the problem—an element which, as we shall see, La Rochefoucauld so notoriously failed to include. A letter from the Duke to Thomas Esprit (*4*, pp. 577-9) suggests that at the outset he did seriously envisage a joint venture with Jacques Esprit, aimed at producing a work that would have resembled *La Fausseté* much more closely than do the *Maximes* as we now have them (see *10*, pp. 7-8). This project, however, appears to have fallen through fairly quickly.

The correspondence between these three individuals (*4*, pp. 541-60) shows them regularly exchanging proposals for maxims (which they refer to as *sentences*) and seeking each other's advice for improving the wording of their inventions. The letters are often jocular in tone, proposing for instance the exchange of a *sentence* for a culinary recipe, but their joint occupation does tend to become obsessive: Mme de Sablé teasingly accuses La Rochefoucauld of having infected her with 'la maladie des sentences', which, it is said elsewhere, 'se gagne comme le rhume'; for his part, the Duke complains to Esprit that 'je suis à la merci des sentences que vous avez suscitées pour troubler mon repos' (*4*, pp. 543, 546, 549, 555, 560). This breezy tone serves to remind us that a *grand seigneur* like

La Rochefoucauld would naturally avoid any suggestion of professionalism or pedantry in pursuing his literary inventions. Yet he was playing the 'game' with an earnestness that he does not always reveal to his partners. An examination of the correspondence proves that the great majority of the proposals came from La Rochefoucauld himself, that in seeking the others' advice he was above all looking for encouragement and approval, and that he took little notice of the comments he received. This collaboration did however produce some confusion as to the authorship of certain texts, so that the 1678 editions of La Rochefoucauld's and Mme de Sablé's *Maximes,* and of Esprit's *Fausseté,* contain a small amount of common material (see *4,* p. xx). But this duplication is exceptional, and from the stylistic point of view there is such a vast difference in quality between most of La Rochefoucauld's productions, and those of Esprit and Sablé—Esprit, for instance, is an extremely verbose writer—that one cannot seriously entertain the idea that the other two contributed anything substantial to our author's masterwork.

Was there ever in fact a *jeu de maximes* in any of the salons? An activity to which such a name might be given formed part of the debates on amorous ethics which are known to have been popular about 1660. This fashion may have been launched by an episode in Part III of Mlle de Scudéry's novel *Clélie,* published in 1658. Various collections of 'questions d'amour' have survived, such as those attributed to Marie Linage (see *9,* pp. 288-300), which pose such questions as: 'Si l'amour est toujours indépendant de la volonté? Si l'amour peut s'accorder avec la prudence? [Cf. La Rochefoucauld's maxim no. 546]. S'il peut y avoir d'éternelles amours?' The answers proposed to such questions were collected and published under the title of *Maximes d'amour,* the most famous collection of which was composed in verse by Bussy-Rabutin. (Here the term *maximes* is used in its then current sense of 'principles, or rules, of conduct', implying nothing about the form or expression.) However there is quite a difference between this kind of salon entertainment and the more private 'game' that was in progress between our three correspondents.

As La Rochefoucauld's proposed maxims were returned to him by his two collaborators, he recorded the texts in a manuscript in which were eventually accumulated some 275 separate items. This register, or a faithful copy of it, forms the document known as 'le manuscrit de Liancourt' which is the most important manuscript source of the *Maximes.* Its contents form the most severely 'Jansenist' presentation that La Rochefoucauld's major work was ever to receive. About 1663, the author had several copies made of it, five of which have survived. (The history of the manuscripts of the *Maximes* is so complicated that no attempt will be made here to summarize it. It has been aptly described as 'un roman policier': see *4*, pp. 383-401 and *30*, pp. 217-25). The purpose of these copies was clearly to conduct a *sondage*—an opinion poll—among Mme de Sablé's acquaintances, in other words among a typical readership sample. This, it was hoped, would assist the author in deciding not only if and when to commit himself to print, but also how, in what form, to publish. Quite a few replies to this 'sondage' have been preserved, in the form of letters addressed to Mme de Sablé, who had organised the operation. The reactions they reveal can be divided roughly into three categories (see *4*, pp. xxi-xxii and 561-77). The first group condemned the *Maximes* as impious, for they denied the reality of the qualities usually held up as Christian virtues. However, another group of equally committed Christians pointed out that in thus savaging humanity, La Rochefoucauld found himself in excellent company, for many of the Fathers of the Church had also denounced such 'false' human virtues. A letter passed on to Mme de Sablé describes the work as 'une école de l'humilité chrétienne, [...] un parfaitement beau commentaire du texte de saint Augustin' (*4*, p. 568). This was more encouraging; but a third body of opinion, while approving the author's intentions, berated him for not making the implied Christian message more explicit (e.g. *ibid.*, p. 574). Clearly all three opinions contained a share of the truth, so it was still up to the author to make his choice.

This wide circulation of maxims in manuscript however produced another, entirely predictable result. Within a few months, a Dutch pirate edition appeared, dated 1664, but it may have been in print before the end of 1663. Though La Rochefoucauld appeared to blame Jacques Esprit for this 'leak' (*4*, p. 578), he has sometimes been suspected of having organised it himself. This is probably unjust, because the edition in question is such an amateurish counterfeit. It has survived in only a few copies, entitled (like the 1663 manuscripts) *Sentences et maximes de morale*. It bears no author's name, merely the imprint *A la Haye, chez Jean et Daniel Steucker*. It contains 188 unnumbered fragments of varying length. There are countless errors of transcription and misprints, and many of the shorter texts found in the 1663 manuscripts have been conflated to produce longer *réflexions* (see *30*, pp. 224-5).

The author, annoyed but less embarrassed than over the 1662 pirate edition of his *Mémoires*, which involved grave political risks, now set about preparing an authentic first edition, which he entrusted to a leading Parisian publisher, Claude Barbin. It bears the title *Réflexions ou sentences et maximes morales*, and the date 1665, though the *achevé d'imprimer* is dated 27 October 1664. This edition contains 318 maxims, briefer on average than those of the Dutch

edition, but still including a relatively large number of the longer
type of *réflexions.*

What account, if any, had La Rochefoucauld taken of the results
of the *sondage?* It has been plausibly argued that because of the
complaints about his alleged attack on 'virtue', he sought deliberately
to give his first edition a new orientation, or at least the appearances
of one. Accordingly he placed at the head of his *recueil* a long,
flamboyant piece on *amour-propre* (no. 563, or the first of the
maximes supprimées) which had first appeared in an anthology five
years earlier, and followed it with three more maxims on the same
topic. At the very end, he added a long, superb *réflexion* on 'le
mépris de la mort' as exhibited by the Stoics (504), one of his most
impressive compositions. Some fifty new maxims were added to
those in the Dutch edition. The text was prefaced by an 'Avis au
lecteur' written in the author's own name, and once again
highlighting the theme of *amour-propre* (the reader being invited to
discard his own before venturing further!).

The undoubted success of the 1665 edition, which was soon sold
out, did not discourage the author from making yet more substantial
alterations to his *recueil.* In the 1666 edition, he discarded sixty
maxims, including the initial piece on *amour-propre,* replacing them
by only forty-four new ones. The 1671, 1675 and 1678 editions, on
the other hand, saw a progressive increase in the number of maxims,
which went up from 302 in 1666 to 504 in 1678. Above all, intensive
stylistic revision, involving in particular the abridgement of many of
the longer *réflexions,* is a feature of each new edition, but especially
of that of 1666. We shall soon be taking a closer look at this process.

Assured of success, the author took even less notice, from 1665
onwards, of hostile comments. The sense of outrage was just as
intense in some quarters after 1665 as at the time of the *sondage.* The
ageing generation of *précieux* seems to have been offended in
particular by La Rochefoucauld's attack on *les belles passions.* His
caustic anti-feminine gibes also aroused some indignation, although
many of the most offensive maxims from this point of view were not
added until the 1670s. From that time dates a letter to the author
himself, from Mme de Rohan, abbesse de Malnoue, who defends her
sex against his witticisms, all the more eloquently for her studied
moderation (*4,* pp. 587-9). As early as 1661, in two letters to Mme
de Sablé, Mme de Maure had declared that La Rochefoucauld 'fait à
l'homme une âme trop laide' (pp. 561-3). A male critic put this point
quite pungently when he complained that the author 'découvrait les
parties honteuses de la vie civile et de la société humaine, sur
lesquelles il fallait tirer le rideau' (p. 572). It was inevitably
suggested that the *Maximes* formed above all a self-portrait of their
author! Even Mme de La Fayette was apparently distressed enough

to lament: 'Quelle corruption il faut avoir dans l'esprit et dans le cœur pour être capable d'imaginer tout cela!' (p. 577). Clearly La Rochefoucauld's slender volume had provoked a furious explosion of comment. If the purpose of the maxim, as he envisaged it, was to stimulate reflection and promote self-discovery, then he had succeeded admirably.

The remaining collection of prose pieces by La Rochefoucauld, so far mentioned only as a title, is the *Réflexions diverses* (*1*, 111-52). It consists of nineteen reflective passages, what we would call short essays, from one paragraph to fifteen in length, on a variety of topics. To these, different editors have added up to five other short pieces, mostly portraits of individuals, including Retz. None of these pieces was printed before 1731, and the last fragment sometimes included, a brief addition to Mme de Sablé's essay 'L'Éducation des enfants' (*1*, p. 152), was not attributed to La Rochefoucauld until 1965. Assigning a precise date to each of them is difficult, except where there is an allusion to recent events (e.g. *1*, pp. 133, 149), but on balance the evidence places their composition in the last seven years of their author's life, i.e. between 1673 and 1680. Most of them present a welcome contrast in style and composition to the *Maximes*, being less aggressive, more expansive and discursive. Some of the longer pieces recall the early *Essais* of Montaigne. As for subject-matter, they may be tentatively placed in four major groups. Seven of them advocate a certain *art de vivre*, being concerned above all with truth, sincerity and harmony between individuals (1-5, 10, 13). Another five (6, 9, 11, 12 and perhaps 15) are showpieces, *morceaux de bravoure*, somewhat baroque in character, being full of paradox, imagery or curious comparisons. Four more come close to the author's preoccupations in the *Maximes*, with their subtle psychological investigations (8, 16, 18, 19), and finally there are three brilliant historical pieces of varying length (7, 14, 17). (Other classifications, on different grounds, might of course be proposed.) Love is predictably a dominant theme, and another recurrent topic is old age (see nos. 9, 15, 18 in particular), which no doubt constitutes another indication of date. Hence the world of the *Réflexions diverses* is markedly different from that of the *Maximes*, though some scholars (e.g. Bénichou, in *13*) have been over-eager to stress the total divergence between the two. We must appreciate their complementarity as well as their opposition.

Imitation and Originality

The question of the originality of the *Maximes* has at times been a vexed one, but it is not too difficult to resolve, given a proper definition of the term in question. If mere resemblances of subject-matter sufficed to convict authors of larceny, La Rochefoucauld's good name would not have survived for long. His contemporaries already accused him of plagiarism. One of Mme de Sablé's correspondents in the *sondage* was particularly severe: 'Cet écrit [...] n'est qu'une collection de plusieurs livres d'où l'on a choisi les sentences, les pointes et les choses qui avaient le plus de rapport au dessein...' (*4*, p. 571). There was one particular source that La Rochefoucauld was quickly accused of exploiting, and that was a work by an English Puritan named Daniel Dyke, eloquently entitled *The Mystery of Self-Deceiving, or a Discourse on the Deceitfulness of Man's Heart*. Published in 1615, it was known in France thanks to a translation of 1634 by the Genevan minister Jean Verneuil, under the title *La Sonde de la conscience*. Its title suggests a major theme of the *Maximes*, but in reality it is much closer to *La Fausseté des vertus humaines*, a fact easily explained by the common source, which is Saint Augustine. In such cases, a number of precise verbal similarities are needed to sustain the charge of plagiarism. Thus it is more constructive to investigate a common 'moral climate' affecting two or more authors, than to hunt for precise 'sources', as for instance Dreyfus-Brisac does in his unconvincing book *La Clef des 'Maximes' de La Rochefoucauld* (1904).

There are however a few authors whose direct influence on the *Maximes* would be difficult to deny. Seneca, the eminent representative of Stoic philosophy, constituted a positive as well as a negative influence. Three maxims, nos. 84, 148 and 511, are close enough in their wording to the Latin of the *De Ira* and the *De Brevitatæ Vitæ* to be considered to be precise reminiscences; other suggested borrowings are vaguer but not implausible. (La Rochefoucauld was no great Latin scholar, but many translations of Seneca existed.) The writer whose influence on the *Maximes* counted most was probably Montaigne. He and La Rochefoucauld had so much in common as men and as authors: a love of paradox and lapidary formulae, and a passionate curiosity about human behaviour in which, despite all the generalisations, the idea of individuality was paramount. Both writers saw human consciousness as being in a state of perpetual flux. Some close verbal parallels have been pointed out between the *Maximes* and statements in the *Essais* such as: 'Les vices s'emploient à la couture de notre liaison, comme les venins à la conservation de notre santé' (Montaigne, III, 1; cf. maxim no. 182). There is however a possible common source for this metaphor in Saint Augustine. Other parallels are equally striking, e.g. Montaigne's formula: 'De quoi se fait la plus subtile folie, que de la plus subtile sagesse?' (II, 12; cf. no. 592) and: 'Se trouve autant de différence de nous à nous-mêmes, que de nous à autrui' (II, 1; cf. no.

135). (Other maxims with a possible source in Montaigne are nos. 23, 169, 256 and 276.)

Another writer from whom La Rochefoucauld borrowed was well known to him thanks to Mme de Sablé, an able Hispanist. About one-third of the *Maximes* published under her name are in fact translations, literal or free, of the aphorisms of Baltasar Gracián, from his *Oráculo manual,* renowned for its harsh judgements on Court society. As for La Rochefoucauld's probable debts to the Spanish writer, they are about a dozen in number, including such often-quoted maxims as nos. 159, 231, 237, 238, 283, 549 and 550. Gracián's 'oracle' was a kind of handbook for ambitious courtiers, to whom it offered some bluntly 'Machiavellian' advice. La Rochefoucauld may well be criticising this aspect of the Spanish author in statements such as the conclusion of no. 117: 'On n'est jamais si aisément trompé que quand on songe à tromper les autres'. (However he goes on to contradict this in no. 118, which is the mirror image of the previous maxim.)

The only other writer who seems to have repeatedly influenced La Rochefoucauld was Jacques Esprit. Such a statement as maxim no, 9, beginning with: 'Les passions ont une injustice et un propre intérêt qui fait qu'il est dangereux de les suivre', is very close to the spirit of *La Fausseté des vertus humaines,* and may indeed have been a fragment 'lost' by Esprit in the course of their initial exchanges (see *4,* p. 9, note 2). Of course, many other 'sources' of individual maxims have been alleged, in Latin prose writers, in Corneille, Descartes, Cureau de la Chambre (author of *Les Caractères des passions,* and a regular visitor at Mme de Sablé's), Bussy-Rabutin and so on. Clear parallels with other, earlier texts have been pointed out in the case of some forty maxims in all—a modest enough figure, surely, out of a total of over six hundred. Even if it were considerably higher, would this matter greatly? The essential originality of La Rochefoucauld lies most often in his choice of words and their patterns, rather than in the ideas expressed. We must indeed look more closely into the nature of the maxim, and all that this implies for the study of a collection such as La Rochefoucauld's.

The Importance of the Maxim Form

The full title given to the *Maximes,* in all editions from 1665 to 1678, was: *Réflexions ou Sentences et Maximes morales.* This is a bit confusing for today's reader, accustomed to distinguishing the briefer *maximes* from the more substantial *réflexions* (a few within the major collection, the rest belonging to the *Réflexions diverses.*) The author himself, on the other hand, appears to equate *réflexions*

with *sentences,* and to distinguish these from *maximes.* In Latin, the
two words had been closely associated in the legal term *maxima
sententia,* or 'authoritative (most general) opinion'. In common
seventeenth-century usage, a *maxime* served a practical purpose: it
was a principle or rule of conduct. A *sentence,* on the other hand,
was thought of as embodying a more 'disinterested' philosophical or
moral truth. It frequently formed the summing-up, the pithy
conclusion to a descriptive, narrative or especially a reflective
passage. According to this definition, the vast majority of the
Maximes are not *maximes*—very few of them offer practical
advice—but *sentences,* and that was the name given to them when
Mme de Sablé conducted her 'sondage'; but usage was evidently
evolving on this point. This tricky area of vocabulary is of course
part of a larger linguistic jungle. How do you distinguish, in English
or in French, between the terms maxim(e), adage, aphorism(e),
apopht(h)egm(e), precept/précepte, reflection/réflexion, epigram/
épigramme and so on? Within this welter of terminology lie various
distinctions of occasion, purpose, content, scope and form.

Whatever we call it, this kind of gnomic expression goes back a
very long way in the annals of humanity. Evidence of man's desire to
express himself in a brief and memorable form is found in the oldest
inscriptions, in the works of the first poets, prophets and
philosophers; also notably, in the pronouncements of oracles.
Aphorisms of various kinds were widely cultivated in Greek and in
Latin, for instance in the field of medicine by Hippocrates, or by
philosophers such as Seneca or historians like Tacitus. As for
popular literature, the didactic use of the proverb or the fable must
go back to the cradle of civilisation; in more recent times, it has
produced variants such as the medieval bestiaries and the sixteenth-
century *Quatrains de Pibrac,* still widely used in education in
Molière's day, so he tells us. At the time of the Renaissance, the most
important contribution to the renewal of the genre was made by the
great humanist scholar, Erasmus. He practised nearly every type of
sententious utterance; brevity and discontinuity were vital, in his
view, in order to distance his works from the over-systematic and
ponderous productions of the pedants. Montaigne's prose likewise
abounds in *sentences* deftly woven into the fabric of the *Essais.* The
didactic use of the maxim was also noteworthy in tragedy: from
Garnier to Corneille, a sententious couplet was used regularly to
conclude a speech containing argument, narrative or even
description. In the printed text, these 'gems of wisdom' were often
highlighted by inverted commas, so that readers could mark, learn
and/or note them down.

The seventeenth century's main role in the development of the
maxim was to provide a climate of refined sociability, in which the

formulation and discussion of abstract truths could flourish. Another development was that not only historians, but authors of personal memoirs—another rapidly expanding genre, especially in the wake of the Fronde—were much inclined to use *sentences*, after the manner of Tacitus, to give an appearance of finality and authority to their conclusions. The *Mémoires* of Retz, in particular, contain a wealth of maxims, and several anthologies of them have been published. Finally, let us not forget one of the most important functions of the maxim at this time, which was for religious meditation and instruction. Innumerable books were published with titles such as *Maximes chrétiennes et morales* or *Sentences et instructions chrétiennes*. Such works provided daily material for pious meditation.

The popularity of the maxim may be put down to its apparent accessibility. The ideal proverb should no doubt combine brevity, clarity and simplicity with some kind of a 'jingle', that is, some memorable arrangement of words. However, the literary variety, the maxim, if it aims above all at brevity and concentration, will inevitably appear, to more sophisticated readers, to over-simplify a complex reality. This may not matter, because, as is the case with contradictory pairs of proverbs, a maxim embodying the opposite truth may seem to be equally valid. One of the attractions of a *sentence* is that, however sweeping its assertions, it cannot annihilate the opposite point of view, that may be enshrined in the preceding or following one. After all, most of our experience is made up, not of logical constructions, but of isolated points of awareness. Yet everyone likes to systematize that experience, in order to make 'sense' of it, and at first glance a good maxim may seem to do just that. However, to the reflective reader, the same maxim may appear incomplete, one-sided, or on the other hand full of hidden implications. This awareness normally incites the reader to reflect further, to try to supply the hidden implication, the missing link in the argument. This kind of 'provocation' may be a vigorous one, if (as often in La Rochefoucauld) the paradox characteristic of the maxim appears too extreme, perhaps even insulting to mankind. A maxim usually involves some sort of comparison; if unexpected, this may be the equivalent of a metaphor, of a 'conceit', even. The effect may be startling, and apparently profound, which will confer a kind of 'oracular' quality on the maxim; but the pronouncements of oracles are notoriously ambiguous. A maxim may appear ambiguous, either because it admits of more than one reasonable interpretation or because it appears to serve two purposes at once, namely moral truth and aesthetic effect. Yet both of these elements are indispensable to the perfect maxim; if either is missing, the result will be moral platitude or gratuitous word-play.

So far we have tended to consider the maxim as an isolated and autonomous statement. In fact it may well form part of a collection, in which case the order of presentation is obviously of some significance. If the disposition appears too logically thematic, the word may take on the appearance of a moral treatise, which is just what the author may have been seeking to avoid. If on the other hand the arrangement appears wholly arbitrary, some readers may find themselves bewildered and discouraged. Once again, a certain compromise seems to be required. The choice, however, is the reader's as well as the author's. In a celebrated article, Roland Barthes has pointed out that there are two ways in which La Rochefoucauld's *Maximes* may be read, what he calls the *pour-moi* and the *pour-soi*; that is, either each one is read in isolation, for its own sake; or consecutively, as a unit in a system of thought. In the first case, it is up to the reader to savour each maxim and appropriate it to himself; in the second, he will be seeking the coherence of a thought-pattern apparently imprisoned in a process of endless repetition (see *11, pp.* 69-70). In the case of La Rochefoucauld, Barthes continues, 'le fruit même du discontinu et du désordre de l'œuvre, c'est que chaque maxime est en quelque sorte, l'archétype de toutes les maximes...' The result, for this critic, is that we must abandon the analytical method for a purely aesthetic approach, 'critique de l'unité sententielle, de son dessin, bref de sa forme: c'est toujours à la maxime, et non aux maximes qu'il faut revenir'. Starobinski, on the other hand, sees intellectual significance in this very same 'disorder' of the *Maximes.* To him, this fragmentation is the mirror of human personality as the author perceives it: 'Leur volontaire désordre, leur aristocratique refus de s'organiser en un système cohérent, constituent une transcription adéquate de la discontinuité interne de l'homme' (*55,* p. 22). Such an appearance of intellectual chaos does not however deter this critic from seeking the overall coherence of the *ensemble.* Each of these opposing points of view may be found stimulating but exaggerated on its own; yet the two are complementary. Faced with a document such as the *Maximes,* everyone would like to make logical sense of it as a whole; but in the course of the investigation, empirical or intuitive methods are more likely to produce satisfactory results than an expectation of rigorous logical coherence.

How much interest did La Rochefoucauld take in the overall 'architecture' of the *Maximes*? What evidence is there of deliberate choice in the ordering of the fragments? This question has provoked much inconclusive discussion by editors and critics. The author apparently believed that the impact of each maxim would be weakened, and the reader perhaps discouraged, if all his variations on the same themes were gathered together. The sucessive prefaces to each edition, and notably to that of 1665, contain a half-hearted apology for the lack of 'order'. So does the *Discours* of La Chapelle-Bessé, who however suggests that 'ce désordre néanmoins a ses grâces' (*4*, pp. 268, 270, 373-4). In compensation, the first readers of the *Maximes* were offered an alphabetical table of contents (pp. 361-6). Yet in 1665 the initial maxims were more obviously grouped in 'clusters' than in any later edition. We distinguish the following themes: *amour-propre* (1-4); passion(s) (5-14); clemency and moderation (15-21); *constance* (22-9); envy and jealousy (30-35); pride (36-41), etc. These groupings become harder to discern as the work advances, and from maxim 250 until the end (317) they are virtually untraceable (see *4*, pp. 283-359). Such 'clusters' are rather less in evidence in the re-arranged parts of the editions from 1666 to 1678, and not at all in the new maxims added on each time at the end. La Rochefoucauld seems to have become more and more persuaded that he should not over-indulge in 'thematic grouping'. As the text stands today, there are plenty of recognisable 'clusters' of maxims, e.g. 68-77, love; 114-29, deception and *finesse;* 143-50, praise and its motives; 213-21, military valour (except 218). It is difficult though to discover any trace of 'argumentative strategy', such as is generally attributed to Pascal, in these groupings, though one or two critics insist on their significance (notably *57*, pp. 218, 220-21). As for choice of diction, the only obvious feature is that with few exceptions La Rochefoucauld varies the constructions used in each successive maxim, in a determined attempt to avoid monotony.

If the author's overall ordering of the fragments was limited in scope, the revision of individual texts, on the other hand, was executed with impressive zeal. In this respect at least, La Rochefoucauld displayed all the thoroughness of a professional man of letters. It was above all in the 1666 edition that he undertook the conversion of many of the longer *réflexions* into the more epigrammatic form of *maximes*. This process involved both excision and condensation (see *3* for complete details). Sometimes one or two sentences are extracted from a longer discursive passage, then modified as required to let them stand on their own (e.g. 65, 88, 192, 198, 254). Even when he does not abridge, the author may achieve a felicitous paraphrase (12), or re-arrangement of the word order (77); and in this process an antithesis, a metaphor or a personfication may emerge with greater clarity (e.g. 32, 40, 44). The revised version may appear more elegant as well as more concise (e.g. 236). Indeed, the 1666 edition produced the definitive version of the majority of the texts in print at that date.

This process of abridgement and condensation inevitably resulted, in many cases, in a further 'hardening' of a form of literary expression that by its very nature tends to appear dogmatic, even aggressive, in its assertions. However, another process at work in these revisions was the insertion of restrictive expressions such as *d'ordinaire, (le plus) souvent, presque, la plupart,* and so on. This process is sometimes represented as an attenuation of the author's harsher moral judgements, even as the result of a 'mellowing' influence attributed to Mme de La Fayette, who is reported to have said of La Rochefoucauld: 'Il m'a donné de l'esprit, mais j'ai réformé son cœur'. Such indeed can easily be the effect of restrictive expressions; but does their inclusion automatically soften the harshness or brighten up the pessimism? Let us consider the case of the epigraph which appears to sum up so well the 'message' of the *Maximes,* though it was not introduced until the 1675 edition: 'Nos vertus ne sont le plus souvent que des vices déguisés'. Here the inclusion of the adverbial expression serves to render acceptable what in its absence might seem too extreme, too provocative a view. Even with the restriction, the maxim remains challenging enough to compel our indignant speculation on the ways in which it might be true—a reaction which the author intends to exploit in the texts that follow. So, as one critic, Corrado Rosso, puts it, such reservations 'augmentent la crédibilité des propositions pessimistes'. A similar but more subtle nuance was introduced into maxims such as no. 83, in which 'L'amitié la plus désintéressée' later became 'Ce que les hommes ont nommé amitié'; and into no. 246, where 'La générosité' was changed to 'Ce qui paraît générosité'. Such restrictions might also be seen as serving a theological purpose which is mentioned in the 1678 Preface, 'Le Libraire au lecteur', where we are assured that the author's strictures apply only to humanity in its present state of 'la nature corrompue par le péché', and are not aimed at 'ceux que Dieu en préserve par une grâce particulière' (*4,* p. 5). In this way, the orthodox Christian point of view could be seen to be respected, albeit in an uncompromising Augustinian form.

By 1666, then, La Rochefoucauld had perfected his technique, and his conception of the maxim had become fully explicit. As a *moraliste,* he has little positive advice to offer: remarkably few texts, a bare dozen at the most, recommend a given form of behaviour within any concrete situation. The normative verb-forms, 'il faut' and 'on doit' are uncommon in the *Maximes.* The author appears to have taken his own observation to heart: 'On donne des conseils, mais on n'inspire pas de conduite' (378). His aim is not to inspire conduct, but to enlighten men about themselves, to initiate them to the study of their own species and to the mechanisms of its behaviour. The fragmentation of the *Maximes* enables the author to harry his readers, to force them to consider a whole series of unflattering comments on human nature. La Rochefoucauld's brand of 'psychological warfare' is less intensive and less systematic than Pascal's, but it was likewise intended to give the reader as little respite as possible.

La Rochefoucauld is a harsh observer, but he does not judge man from a position of Olympian detachment. The most frequently used personal pronoun is *nous*: it appears 147 times in the 504 maxims of 1678. This pronoun, however, can be slightly ambiguous. La Rochefoucauld wrote to Thomas Esprit in 1664, soon after the publication of the Dutch edition of the *Maximes*: 'Quant je dis *nous*, j'entends parler de l'homme qui croit ne devoir qu'à lui seul ce qu'il a de bon' (*4*, p. 578). However, whenever this *nous* is opposed to *autrui* or to *les autres,* it reveals antagonisms within the human race; this cleavage underlines the interpersonal dimensions of the passions that La Rochefoucauld studies.

Literary perfection is clearly an aid to the propagation of the message, but La Rochefoucauld pursued this goal with an enthusiasm that suggests a considerable investment of his own *amour-propre* in his enterprise. His twin objectives of psychological truth and artistic excellence will continue to share the honours throughout the successive editions of the *Maximes*. This constant dual purpose emerges clearly, for instance, if we compare the epigraph of 1675-1678 with the longer maxim which it replaced:

> Nos vertus ne sont le plus souvent que des vices déguisés.

> Nous sommes si préoccupés en notre faveur, que souvent ce que nous prenons pour des vertus n'est que des vices qui leur ressemblent, et que l'amour-propre nous déguise. (607)

The 'true' maxim here is the epigraph: it represents the 'prompt' which should encourage the reader to produce an explanation of the paradox, perhaps in terms that will resemble those of the longer, rejected passage. What Jean Lafond has called the 'non-dit' is an important dimension of the *Maximes*. La Rochefoucauld, so far as his readers are concerned, has perfected the art of conversation as he describes it in the fourth of his *Réflexions diverses*: 'Il y a de l'habileté à n'épuiser pas les sujets qu'on traite, et à laisser toujours quelque chose à penser et à dire' (*1*, p. 117). Could La Fontaine have read this unpublished text before he wrote his *Discours à Monsieur le Duc de la Rochefoucault* (*Fables*, X, 14, published in 1679)? He echoes its thought with remarkable precision:

> ... et tiens qu'il faut laisser
> Dans les plus beaux sujets quelque chose à penser.

Chapter Two

The Demolition of Man

It was once accepted by all that La Rochefoucauld had a 'system', quite a simple one, with a single key to unlock it. This idea was first put forward by La Bruyère, less than a decade after our author's death:

> Observant que l'amour-propre est dans l'homme la cause de tous ses faibles, [il] l'attaque sans cesse, quelque part où il le trouve; et cette unique pensée, comme multipliée en mille manières différentes, a toujours, par le choix des mots et la variété de l'expression, la grâce de la nouveauté. ('Discours sur Théophraste')

Seventy years later, Voltaire wrote more or less the same thing, though he did give La Rochefoucauld some credit for mental ingenuity as well as for stylistic resourcefulness:

> Quoiqu'il n'y ait qu'une vérité dans ce livre, qui est que l'amour-propre est le mobile de tout, cependant cette pensée se présente sous tant d'aspects variés, qu'elle est presque toujours piquante. (*Le Siècle de Louis XIV*)

Modern criticism has tended to question or even to reject the notion of a 'system' dominating the work of La Rochefoucauld. W.G. Moore, for instance, writes that 'the thinking behind the *Maximes* is of course unsystematic', and adds 'Thank goodness' (*45*, p. 65). In fact everyone can be said to have grasped at least a part of the truth. We do find a 'system' in the *Maximes,* but it is far from being a water-tight construction, and it does not fit the whole of the reality that La Rochefoucauld is attempting, for the most part unsystematically, to describe (see *30*, pp. 21-5, 173-5).

This 'system' is well summed up in the by now familiar epigraph: 'Nos vertus ne sont le plus souvent que des vices déguisés'. Here we find both the author's central theme, and his technique of 'reductive definition', signalled by the *ne ... que* construction, which recurs eighty-one times in the text of the *Maximes*. True virtues may exist, but they are rare, and difficult to distinguish from the false virtues that ape them. 'Il est difficile de juger si un procédé net, sincère et honnête est un effet de probité ou d'habileté' (170). Here La Rochefoucauld is uncompromising: if virtue is impure, then he will not acknowledge it as virtue. As a *moraliste,* he saw his essential task as one of unmasking. In the Frontispiece of 1665 (*1*, p. 23), the author is represented as a cherub bearing the title 'l'amour de la vérité'. He has removed a mask bearing a serene expression from the head of a philosopher, revealing an ugly, tormented face beneath. The philosopher in question is Seneca, who himself had claimed to unmask his fellow men—a task some modern critics also see themselves as performing at the expense of La Rochefoucauld! Unmasking, as Starobinski observes, appears to be the speciality of the *moraliste* (*54*, pp. 33-4).

The 'system' or unmasking process consists essentially of passing all conventionally acknowledged virtues in review, in order to redefine them in less flattering terms. What La Rochefoucauld calls 'les vertus apparentes' are shown to be 'les vertus décevantes'. Man is castigated, even in his noblest aspirations: 'L'amour de la justice n'est, en la plupart des hommes, que la crainte de souffrir l'injustice' (78; cf. 579), and in all his seemingly disinterested impulses, such as gratitude: 'Il en est de la reconnaissance comme de la foi des marchands: elle entretient le commerce...' (223; cf. 225, 298). Friendship, a topic much discussed in Mme de Sablé's entourage, is similarly manhandled by La Rochefoucauld:

> Ce que les hommes ont nommé amitié n'est qu'une société, qu'un ménagement réciproque d'intérêts, et qu'un échange de bons offices; ce n'est enfin qu'un commerce où l'amour-propre se propose toujours quelque chose à gagner. (83)

The recurrent mercantile vocabulary is used to undermine the very notion of disinterestedness. (Note again, however, that it is not the virtue itself, but man's miserable counterfeiting of it, that is under attack.) A further discreditable aspect of friendship is revealed in another maxim: 'Nous nous consolons aisément des disgrâces de nos amis, lorsqu'elles servent à signaler notre tendresse pour eux' (235; cf. 583). It is our display of concern that matters to us, rather than our friend's welfare. If friendship is eternally suspect, then what of love? 'Si l'on juge de l'amour par la plupart de ses effets, il ressemble plus à la haine qu'à l'amitié' (72; cf. 262). These 'false virtues' dominate society at large, and its rulers, as well as the conduct of individuals. The mercy shown by monarchs, such as Corneille's Auguste, is often a sham: 'La clémence des princes n'est souvent qu'une politique pour gagner l'affection des peuples' (15; cf. 16). It is this kind of semi-voluntary or involuntary deception that holds society together: 'Les hommes ne vivraient pas longtemps en société, s'ils n'étaient les dupes les uns des autres' (87). The same technique of 'reductive definition' enables La Rochefoucauld to call into question the whole conventional notion of sincerity: 'La sincérité est une ouverture du cœur. On la trouve en fort peu de gens, et celle que l'on voit d'ordinaire n'est qu'une fine dissimulation, pour attirer la confiance des autres' (62). In other circumstances, it is vanity, even more than self-interest, that motivates our sincerity: 'L'envie de parler de nous, et de faire voir nos défauts du côté que nous voulons bien les montrer, fait une grande partie de notre sincérité' (383). Many such variations, on this and other themes, could be quoted.

All these examples of La Rochefoucauld's 'system' involve some investigation of motive. His verdict is nearly always determined by his estimate of the motive that appears to have prompted the action. Such an 'ethics of intention' is central to the Augustinian tradition of moral judgement, according to which the very same action will be considered virtuous, if it is inspired by charity, but sinful if some self-centred impulse can be shown to have been responsible. But motivation is not always that simple to judge. What La Rochefoucauld is quite often saying is that there are in practice no simple moral values, because there are no simple psychological states, in which a given quality or motive is not mixed with another, perhaps very different one. Two of our author's best-known similes serve to convey this notion of complex, obscure motivation, and its consequences for our moral judgements: 'Les vertus se perdent dans l'intérêt, comme les fleuves se perdent dans la mer' (171); and 'Les vices entrent dans la composition des vertus, comme les poisons entrent dans la composition des remèdes' (182). True virtue must be spontaneous, for as soon as we stop to ponder on our actions, we may question the purity of our motives. As Jean Lafond puts it: 'C'est cet écart entre la vertu en soi et notre réalité psychologique qui fait, dans la morale de La Rochefoucauld, toute la difficulté d'être, et d'être vrai' (*30*, p. 11).

Despite these complexities, La Rochefoucauld's description of man is founded on one basic concept, namely *l'amour-propre*. The word itself is used only twenty-one times in the text of the 640-odd *Maximes,* but the presence of the idea can be sensed almost everywhere. As a theological concept, *amour-propre* goes right back to St Augustine's *De Civitate Dei (City of God),* written in the early fifth century A.D. The vision of man in this work, indeed its whole structure, rests upon the opposition between the two loves which contend for mastery of the human soul: *amor Dei* or charity, on which is founded the City of God, the Celestial Jerusalem; and *amor sui* or self-love, the source of concupiscence or worldly desire, on which stands Babylon, the City of Mammon. La Rochefoucauld, with his halting Latin, had certainly read neither St Augustine nor Jansen's *Augustinus,* which also contains a long disquisition on *amor sui.* He is more likely to have acquainted himself with the subject in conversations with Jacques Esprit, or through the more accessible works in French of another learned theologian of the Oratoire, Le Père Senault. At the onset of his extended 'portrait' of *amour-propre* (563), he proposes a recognisably Augustinian definition, namely: 'l'amour de soi-même et de toutes choses pour soi'; but he does not distinguish, as did many later thinkers, between sinful *amour-propre* and *amour de soi-même,* a more 'legitimate' kind of self-esteem and self-preservation. In fact he amalgamates the two, for the concept of 'self-preservation' is very much present, as we shall see, in his description of *amour-propre.*

In the *Maximes,* this term has lost its explicit theological overtones, but as a psychological concept, *amour-propre* is present everywhere, named or unnamed, since all human activity appears to be rooted in this all-pervasive form of egoism. It is 'le plus grand des flatteurs' (2), for it is 'plus habile que le plus habile homme du monde' (4). It dominates every facet of our lives, for 'nous ne pouvons rien aimer que par rapport à nous' (81). It is present even in the most apparently disinterested forms of devotion and kindness, as the author affirms with the aid of another mercantile metaphor:

> Il semble que l'amour-propre soit la dupe de la bonté, et qu'il s'oublie lui-même lorsque nous travaillons pour l'avantage des autres; cependant c'est prendre le chemin le plus assuré pour arriver à ses fins; c'est prêter à usure, sous prétexte de donner; c'est enfin s'acquérir tout le monde par un moyen subtil et délicat. (236)

The most self-regarding passion of all is the one we call 'love': 'Il n'y a point de passion où l'amour de soi-même règne si puissamment que dans l'amour, et on est toujours plus disposé à sacrifier le repos de ce qu'on aime qu'à perdre le sien' (262). Even when we mourn the loss of our loved ones, we are not really mourning them, but ourselves: 'nous pleurons la diminution de notre bien, de notre plaisir, de notre considération' (233). It is not only inborn but inbred: 'L'éducation que l'on donne d'ordinaire aux jeunes gens est un second amour-propre qu'on leur inspire' (261). Man's various passions are depicted as 'les divers goûts de l'amour-propre' (531).

Two other key terms in the psychology of the *Maximes* are intimately bound up with this concept of universal egoism. We normally try to conceal our own *amour-propre,* in so far as we are aware of it. Whenever we give up the attempt, the result is the uninhibited display of our pride. *L'orgueil,* according to a passage in the *Réflexions diverses (1,* p. 150) is 'inséparable de l'amour-propre'. It is indeed, like self-love, the common property of all mankind: 'L'orgueil est égal dans tous les hommes, et il n'y a de différence qu'aux moyens et à la manière de mettre au jour' (35). La Rochefoucauld adds, with caustic irony, that it is Nature's gift to human frailty, for it gently closes our eyes to all our imperfections (36). Yet it is also the source of our ingratitude, which can cause us even to hate those to whom we have too great an obligation (14). Pride and *amour-propre* each play a complementary role in producing that ingratitude: 'L'orgueil ne veut pas devoir, et l'amour-propre ne veut pas payer' (228). In a fine example of the stage metaphor, La Rochefoucauld distinguishes between two types of pride:

> L'orgueil, comme lassé de ses artifices et de ses différentes métamorphoses, après avoir joué tout seul tous les personnages de la comédie humaine, se montre avec un visage naturel, et se découvre par la fierté: de sorte qu'à proprement parler, la fierté est l'éclat et la déclaration de l'orgueil. (568)

The principal cluster of maxims describing pride (33-37) is followed by a group of three more on another theme clearly associated with that of *amour-propre,* namely *intérêt.* This also produces contrasting effects in different individuals: 'L'intérêt, qui aveugle les uns, fait la lumière des autres' (40), and like its companion *amour-propre,* it can take on the mask of its own opposite: 'L'intérêt parle toutes sortes de langues, et joue toutes sortes de personnages, même celui de désintéressé' (39). It is the binding force of our friendships, particularly with persons of higher rank (85). In a judgement remarkable for its all-embracing intransigence, La Rochefoucauld asserts that 'on ne loue jamais personne sans intérêt' (144). Self-interest has few scruples in its choice of means: 'Le nom de la vertu sert à l'intérêt aussi utilement que les vices' (187). *Intérêt* shares with *vertu* the rank of fourth most frequently-used noun in the *Maximes,* according to Jean de Bazin's *Vocabulaire* (Nizet, 1967). The inseparable links between *intérêt* and *amour-propre* form the theme of one of the most remarkable of the longer maxims, a masterpiece of what might be called ''hyperbolic animation', depicting man as a kind of automaton, normally inert but sometimes galvanized by passion:

> L'intérêt est l'âme de l'amour-propre, de sorte que comme le corps, privé de son âme, est sans vue, sans ouïe, sans connaissance, sans sentiment et sans mouvement, de même, l'amour-propre séparé, s'il le faut dire ainsi, de son intérêt, ne voit, n'entend, ne sent et ne se remue plus. De là vient qu'un même homme, qui court la terre et les mers pour son intérêt, devient soudainement paralytique pour l'intérêt des autres; de là vient ce soudain assoupissement et cette mort que nous causons à tous ceux à qui nous contons nos affaires; de là vient leur prompte résurrection lorsque, dans notre narration, nous y mêlons quelque chose qui les regarde: de sorte que nous voyons, dans nos conversations et dans nos traités, que, dans un même moment, un homme perd connaissance et revient à soi, selon que son propre intérêt s'approche de lui, ou qu'il s'en retire. (510)

When pride ceases to lend dignity to our self-interest, it gives way to envy (281), a malignant force which La Rochefoucauld paints in hideous colours. The universal nature of envy is asserted in an ironical formulation: 'Il y a encore plus de gens sans intérêt que sans envie' (486). But our envy is usually well-concealed, for it is 'une passion timide et honteuse que l'on n'ose jamais avouer' (27). It is nonetheless violent, being 'une fureur qui ne peut souffrir le bien des autres' (28; cf. 280) and 'plus irréconciliable que la haine' (328). A proof of inborn superiority would be its absence (433); a fortunate state indeed, for envy, once established, is almost ineradicable: 'Notre envie dure toujours plus longtemps que le bonheur de ceux que nous envions' (476).

With all its ramifications and sinister relatives, *amour-propre* in La Rochefoucauld is not an easy concept to delimit and define. Where does it begin, and where does it end? Is it an evil force, a supreme tempter that leads men astray? Or is it not somehow consubstantial with the human consciousness that is being led astray? How can such a thing as 'self-love' come to hate itself, and perform other contortions, as in no. 563? This fascinating passage begins with a theological definition of *amour-propre* as 'anti-charity'—the exact reverse of the Catechism definition of charity—but at once its subject is transformed into an autonomous being, invested with all the perceptions of the human mind and all the functions of the human will. According to Jean Lafond, 'Il est la force mauvaise, la force *perverse,* qui nous fait nous détacher du Créateur pour lui préférer la créature; mais il est aussi cette donnée immédiate, inscrite dans notre être biologique lui-même, qui nous constitue comme individu' (*30,* pp. 178-81. For further discussion of this concept, see *21, 31, 40,* and *60*). La Rochefouauld's awesomely 'baroque' description of *amour-propre* as a kind of legendary monster serves to encompass all the potential contradictions in his conception of it. (This piece was published five years before any other text in the *Maximes,* in a *Recueil de pièces en prose,* late in 1659 or early in 1660. It was dedicated, most curiously, to a nun, Mlle d'Épernon, who in 1657 had herself spectacularly rejected the lure of *amour-propre* by taking the veil, at a time when she might have married into the Polish royal family.)

The 'mythical metamorphosis' of *amour-propre* begins in the second sentence of no. 563, with a comparison between its indefatigable activity and that of the bee darting from flower to flower, 'pour en tirer ce qui lui est propre'. *Amour-propre* is revealed at once as a Protean being, in a state of constant transformation:

> Rien n'est si impétueux que ses désirs; rien de si caché que ses desseins, rien de si habile que ses conduites; ses souplesses ne se peuvent représenter, ses transformations passent celles des métamorphoses, et ses raffinements ceux de la chimie. On ne peut sonder la profondeur, ni percer les ténèbres de ses abîmes: là il est à

> couvert des yeux les plus pénétrants; il y fait mille insensibles tours et
> détours; là il est souvent invisible à lui-même; il y conçoit, il y nourrit et
> il y élève, sans le savoir, un grand nombre d'affections et de haines; il
> en forme de si monstrueuses que, lorsqu'il les a mises au jour, il les
> méconnaît, ou il ne peut se résoudre à les avouer.

Its perspicacity concerning the world without is matched only by its
ignorance of the world within: 'en quoi il est semblable à nos yeux,
qui découvrent tout et sont aveugles seulement pour eux-mêmes.'
The author thus gradually constructs his 'portrait' of a self-
devouring and self-contradicting monster, whose existence is
governed by only one law, that of survival. There is a probable
allusion to the dedicatee's religious vocation, though possibly also to
the Jansenists, in the reference to the presence of *amour-propre* in
the 'enemy camp':

> Il passe même dans le parti des gens qui lui font la guerre, il entre dans
> leurs desseins, et ce qui est admirable, il se hait lui-même avec eux, il
> conjure sa perte, il travaille même à sa ruine; enfin il ne se soucie que
> d'être, et pourvu qu'il soit, il veut bien être son ennemi.

In this reference to the survival instincts of *amour-propre,* the
modern reader may see an anticipation of later concepts of a life
force, an *élan vital.* (In fact *amour-propre*—the concept if not the
word—is identified with self-preservation in the writings of La
Rochefoucauld's great English contemporary, Thomas Hobbes.)
How seriously we are meant to take this piece is a moot point. It was
first published in an anthology to be read for entertainment, and it
may not have been greatly appreciated by its first readers, since the
author dropped it altogether from 1666 onwards. Nevertheless, this
remarkable 'portrait' links up with some of the *Réflexions diverses;*
in particular, its concluding simile is taken up again in no. 6,
entitled 'De l'amour et de la mer'. There is quite a contrast between
the obvious self-indulgence of this passage, and the moral and
intellectual rigour of Pascal's equally celebrated fragment on
amour-propre (*Pensées,* ed. Lafuma, 978). Yet Pascal's devastatingly
direct message is basically the same as La Rochefoucauld's:
'L'homme n'est donc que déguisement, que mensonge et hypocrisie,
et en soi-même, et à l'égard des autres'.
  This memorable 'portrait' therefore depicts *amour-propre* as a
creature possessed of a ferocious will, or appetite, and yet strangely
benighted, ignorant in particular of the murky recesses of its own
consciousness. For all his zeal in denouncing hypocrisy in its various
forms, La Rochefoucauld finds conscious deception rather less
interesting that the notion of involuntary, or half-voluntary, self-
deception. This process was located in a 'grey area'—the
unconscious, as we would now call it—that thinking men in the

early or mid-seventeenth century were only just beginning to investigate. The idea of self-deception recommended itself to moralists of the Puritan or Jansenist persuasion, for it enabled them, despite their belief in man's total corruption, to explain the existence of individuals whose 'virtue' seemed to set an example to their fellow men. Daniel Dyke's treatise, it will be recalled, was entitled *The Mystery of Self-Deceiving*. One effect of *amour-propre* is that man, the great deceiver, becomes an expert at deceiving himself as well as others, setting in motion a complex social charade revolving around the theme of *le trompeur trompé* (see *42*, pp. 105-107; *47*, pp. 46-8)

The theme of self-deception is taken up enthusiastically by La Rochefoucauld. He stresses man's lack of intimate self-knowledge: 'Il s'en faut bien que nous connaissions toutes nos volontés' (295; cf. 460). Elsewhere he puts the dilemma in more everyday terms: 'Comment peut-on répondre de ce qu'on voudra à l'avenir, puisque l'on ne sait pas précisément ce que l'on veut dans le temps présent?' (575) Self-knowledge becomes difficult to achieve when one part of our personality is a stranger to the other: 'Tous ceux qui connaissent leur esprit ne connaissent pas leur cœur' (103), and as a result, 'L'esprit est toujours la dupe du cœur' (102; cf. 43). At least, when the deceiver is one's own self, this is less injurious to one's pride: 'On ne se peut consoler d'être trompé pas ses ennemis et trahi par ses amis, et l'on est souvent satisfait de l'être par soi-même' (114; cf. 115). The more we attempt to dissimulate before others, the less attention we give to scrutinizing our own motives: 'Nous sommes si accoutumés à nous déguiser aux autres, qu'enfin nous nous déguisons à nous-mêmes' (119; cf. 516). An element of self-deception is found in some of the more complex psychological situations which La Rochefoucauld describes, for instance in the state of mind of the bereaved: 'Ainsi les morts ont l'honneur des larmes qui ne coulent que pour les vivants. Je dis que c'est une espèce d'hypocrisie, à cause que dans ces sortes d'afflictions, on se trompe soi-même.' Small wonder, though, that we tend to lose our bearings in these subtle gradations of feeling and motive: On pleure pour avoir la réputation d'être tendre; on pleure pour être plaint; on pleure pour être pleuré; enfin on pleure pour éviter la honte de ne pleurer pas' (233).

By thus exploring the obscure frontier between conscious and unconscious motivation, La Rochefoucauld is able once again to call into question the whole concept of sincerity. The mask becomes progressively indistinguishable from the face below. This opposition between *être* and *paraître* is undoubtedly one of the major themes of the *Maximes,* perhaps the dominant one, though not always the most explicit. Clearly, there is still a long way to go between La

Rochefoucauld and Freud; but here and there in the *Maximes* we find an allusion to something resembling a state of 'submerged consciousness' in which the self-deception is at least half-voluntary (236; cf. 582), the motivation being identifiable yet not fully conscious (see *42*, pp. 99-100). We are not so far away, either, from the existentialist concept of *mauvaise foi,* that semi-voluntary state of self-deception prompted by the desire for personal comfort or advantage. Our author's probings into the realm of *l'inconscient* are penetrating enough to have interested such an expert in this field as Jacques Lacan, who has proposed some original interpretations of a few maxims (see *18*, pp. 212-14). On the other hand, La Rochefoucauld has been attacked by Sartre (in *La Transcendance de l'ego*) for establishing 'egotistic activity' on a subconscious level, and above all, somewhat intemperately, by Francis Jeanson (*Les Temps modernes* [1950] pp. 1764-96; reprinted in *Lignes de départ* [1963] pp. 71-107). Here our author is reproached for 'mauvaise foi' in seeking to propound general laws of behaviour from which he implicitly exempts himself—a highly debatable claim (see *42*, pp. 87-92).

Whether he was a true pioneer explorer of *l'inconscient* or not, La Rochefoucauld contributed powerfully to the overthrow of a certain conception of man, proposing in its place what W.G. Moore has called 'une nouvelle anthropologie'. In the Aristotelian view inherited by the Scholastic philosophers, man was an enlightened creature capable of rational behaviour, even of 'magnanimity', thanks to his self-knowledge and free will. The notion of self-deception involved in the functioning of *amour-propre* challenged these assumptions, though it did not imply the abandonment of rational methods of investigation. On the contrary, reason was the very instrument that served to dethrone reason. La Rochefoucauld sometimes marshals all his analytical subtlety in order to voice his distrust of reason, and of its companion *prudence* or 'practical wisdom': 'Il n'y a point d'éloges qu'on ne donne à la prudence; cependant elle ne saurait nous assurer du moindre événement' (65). This maxim began in the Liancourt manuscript as a much longer, eloquent disquisition on man's elevation of *prudence* to almost divine status, in the face of true Divine wisdom as conceived of in Christian doctrine. It was whittled down from edition to edition, and finally to this brief uncompromising assertion. Speculative reason is no more kindly treated in the *Maximes* than practical *prudence* (e.g. in no. 106). Indeed, reason seems to be of little use to us in our striving, not just for knowledge, but for self-improvement: 'La fortune nous corrige de plusieurs défauts que la raison ne saurait corriger' (154—*plusieurs,* in the French of La Rochefoucauld's day, was often still the equivalent of *beaucoup*.) It is *amour-propre* that

is more likely to give us effective insight into our own minds (e.g.
494). Even when reason does provide the sagacity we need, we lack
the strength of will required to follow its commands: 'Nous n'avons
pas assez de force pour suivre toute notre raison' (42). Maltreated
more often than not, man's rational faculty does emerge, as we shall
see, with a few consolation prizes, especially in the *Réflexions
diverses*.

Far from committing the gross over-simplification implied in
summary accounts of his 'system', La Rochefoucauld is sometimes
lost in wonder at the complexity of human nature, at the multiplicity
and ambiguity of the motives that appear to govern men's
behaviour. 'L'imagination ne saurait inventer tant de diverses
contrariétés qu'il y en a naturellement dans le cœur de chaque
personne', he exclaims (478), giving as an example: 'On ne saurait
compter toutes les espèces de vanité' (506). Faced with a single
blanket concept describing an aspect of personality, he sometimes
applies a dissection technique which splits up the general notion into
its component parts, carefully marking its various facets and
gradations. This technique is naturally reserved for some of the
more extended passages in the *Maximes*. It is exhibited to perfection
in no. 215, dedicated to forms of courage and cowardice on the
battlefield; and in no. 233, on bereavement, the theme of which is
neatly encapsulated in the opening sentence: 'Il y a dans les
afflictions diverses sortes d'hypocrisie'. The infinite variety of
human personality is evoked in such *réflexions* as these. Elsewhere
it is the instability of the individual consciousness that forms the
theme: 'Il y a dans le cœur humain une génération perpétuelle de
passions, en sorte que la ruine de l'une est presque toujours
l'établissement d'une autre.' (10) In this incessant process of
gestation, each passion tends to produce its opposite (11). An early
version of no. 65 contained an eloquent phrase describing man's
essential mutability: 'une matière aussi changeante et inconnue qu'est
l'homme.' So elusive is the self, so unstable the passions, that
adequate self-knowledge becomes almost unattainable. The central
core, the innermost recess, of man's enigmatic being is designated
by La Rochefoucauld, as by Pascal, by the term *le cœur*. In its most
characteristic uses in the *Maximes,* this word has very different
overtones from its present-day ones, though there are exceptions
(e.g. 175, 315, 346, 484). Its particular connotation here reflects an
Augustinian view of fallen man's personality: *le cœur* is the
mysterious vessel in which takes place the 'génération perpétuelle de
passions'; it is the seat of *amour-propre* in all its monstrous forms;
it is the place where man's consciousness seems to merge
mysteriously with his physical being. It depths are quite beyond our
ken, and may hold unexpected secrets. The only pure love known to

humanity is 'celui qui est caché au fond du cœur, et que nous
ignorons nous-mêmes' (69)—the subconscious, it would seem, being
the seat of authentic feeling. Intellect can never match the
resourcefulness of *le cœur* (102, 103, 108). In an allusion to his
commitment as a writer, La Rochefoucauld refers to 'les maximes
qui découvrent le cœur de l'homme' (524).

The ceaseless drive of *amour-propre* may suggest a certain
strength of personality as the human norm. La Rochefoucauld,
however, seems equally convinced of man's negative characteristics,
to which he refers under the twin heading of *faiblesse* and *paresse*.
The first forms part of what might be called a psychic dialectic: 'Les
passions en engendrent souvent qui leur sont contraires: l'avarice
produit quelquefois la prodigalité, et la prodigalité l'avarice; on est
souvent ferme par faiblesse, et audacieux par timidité' (11). This
notion at least enables the author to show a little indulgence—if it
really is indulgence—towards humanity in its frailty: 'L'on fait plus
souvent des trahisons par faiblesse que par un dessein formé de
trahir' (120; cf. 122). Beside *amour-propre,* this 'inert matter'
forms part of the immoveable bedrock of man's nature: 'La
faiblesse est le seul défaut que l'on ne saurait corriger' (130). The
mind has its own particular 'weakness', which consists of agreeing
with all opinions in turn (181). In a particularly challenging
assertion, La Rochefoucauld condemns as worthless humane
qualities of a negative kind, that is, those that may simply be the
product of a weak personality: 'Nul ne mérite d'être loué de bonté,
s'il n'a pas la force d'être méchant: toute autre bonté n'est le plus
souvent qu'une paresse ou une impuissance de la volonté' (237; cf.
479, 481). (Once again the moral judgement is directed at the source
of the action, at the motive or the cause, rather than at its effects.)
Such 'weakness' is particularly blameworthy because its inhibits
intellectual honesty and self-knowledge: 'Les personnes faibles ne
peuvent être sincères' (316). Under its influence, we are perpetually
inclined to take the line of least resistance, and readily to accept our
misfortunes as inevitable (325). So deleterious are its effects, as seen
by La Rochefoucauld, that eventually he declares: 'La faiblesse est
plus opposée à la vertu que le vice' (445).

If 'weakness' is an abiding human trait, some of its intermittent
manifestations fall under the heading of *paresse,* which is depicted as
a malignant cancer in man's nature. One of the most eloquent of the
longer maxims drives this point home:

> C'est se tromper que de croire qu'il n'y a que les violentes passions,
> comme l'ambition et l'amour, qui puissent triompher des autres. La
> paresse, toute languissante qu'elle est, ne laisse pas d'en être souvent la
> maîtresse: elle usurpe sur tous les desseins et sur toutes les actions de la

vie; elle y détruit et y consume insensiblement les passions et les vertus.
(266)

This vice provides the true explanation of some rather negative
virtues: 'La modération ne peut avoir le mérite de combattre
l'ambition et de la soumettre: elles ne se trouvent jamais ensemble.
La modération est la langueur et la paresse de l'âme, comme
l'ambition en est l'activité et l'ardeur' (293; cf. 169). Of all our
vices, it is the one we most readily confess to (398); yet mental sloth
is the most insidious kind of *paresse*: 'L'esprit s'attache par paresse et
par constance à ce qui lui est facile et agréable: cette habitude met
toujours des bornes à nos connaissances, et jamais personne ne s'est
donné la peine d'étendre et de conduire son esprit aussi loin qu'il
pourrait aller' (482). (This maxim constitutes an impressive
declaration of faith in the potential of human intelligence.) The
origin of *la paresse* is presumed to be diabolical (512). Mme de Sablé
wrote to Mme de Schomberg that 'L'auteur a trouvé dans son
humeur la maxime de la paresse, car jamais il n'y en a eu une si
grande que la sienne' (*4*, p. 567, n. 18). Although La Rochefoucauld
does not admit to this charge in his self-portrait, there is a text, one
of the most unusual and memorable in the *Maximes,* which may lend
it some credibility. It is one by which the critic Paul Martin (finding
in it a Mallarmean 'insolite mystère') pronounces himself fascinated
(*L'Information littéraire,* 1983, p. 115). That it produced such an
effect on him is hardly surprising, for La Rochefoucauld, beginning
on a note of apparently severe Christian disapproval for this sin,
gradually 'weakens' and leads us, through a progression of
suggestive images, to a final declaration of surrender:

> De toutes les passions, celle qui est la plus inconnue à nous-mêmes,
> c'est la paresse; elle est la plus ardente et la plus maligne de toutes,
> quoique sa violence soit insensible, et que les dommages qu'elle cause
> soient très cachés. Si nous considérons très attentivement son pouvoir,
> nous verrons qu'elle se rend en toutes rencontres maîtresse de nos
> sentiments, de nos intérêts et de nos plaisirs; c'est la rémore qui a la
> force d'arrêter les plus grands vaisseaux; c'est une bonace plus
> dangereuse aux plus importantes affaires que les écueils et les plus
> grandes tempêtes. Le repos de la paresse est un charme secret de l'âme
> qui suspend soudainement les plus ardentes poursuites et les plus
> opiniâtres résolutions; pour donner enfin la véritable idée de cette
> passion, il faut dire que la paresse est comme une béatitude de l'âme,
> qui la console de toutes ses pertes, et qui lui tient lieu de tous les biens.
> (630)

To grant such a prominent role among the passions to sloth is to
underline the importance of the physical factors which weigh down
upon men's existence. Among these, La Rochefoucauld gives pride of
place to *l'humeur.* Seventeenth-century medicine was still dominated

by the ancient theory of the humours, according to which the various 'temperaments' or 'complexions' were determined by the particular combination within one individual of the four bodily 'humours': blood, phlegm, bile or choler, and black bile or melancholy. Our author could have found this theory ably expounded, for instance, in the treatise *Les Caractères des passions* by one of Mme de Sablé's *habitués*, Martin Cureau de la Chambre. According to the *Maximes*, some of men's most prestigious achievements are to be explained thus: 'Ces grandes et éclatantes actions qui éblouissent les yeux sont représentées par les politiques comme les effets des grands desseins, au lieu que ce sont d'ordinaire les effets de l'humeur et des passions' (7). The natural contentment enjoyed by certain individuals is of the same nature: 'La modération des personnes heureuses vient du calme que la bonne fortune donne à leur humeur' (17). Average humanity can strive to overcome its effects with some hope of success, but 'les fous et les sottes gens ne voient que par leur humeur' (414). Of the various types of courage that La Rochefoucauld so carefully distinguishes (215), he declares: 'Il n'y a pas moins de différence entre elles qu'entre les visages et les humeurs'. Such physical influences determine our individual talents and aptitudes: 'La complexion qui fait le talent pour les petites choses est contraire à celle qui fait le talent des grandes' (569). Together with *amour-propre, l'humeur* constitutes the internal force which shapes men's lives, as opposed to the external factor referred to as *la fortune*. These two are several times associated in the *Maximes*, indeed to such an extent that 'la fortune et l'humeur gouvernent le monde' (435; cf. 545, 47, 61).

In another maxim, La Rochefoucauld is even more explicit in identifying the physical origin of our psychic experience:

> Les humeurs du corps ont un cours ordinaire et réglé, qui meut et qui tourne imperceptiblement notre volonté; elles roulent ensemble, et exercent successivement un empire secret en nous, de sorte qu'elles ont une part considérable à toutes nos actions, sans que nous le puissions connaître. (297)

There is a suggestion here that the body will not easily yield the secrets of these occult activities. This description of the 'cours ordinaire et réglé' of the humours is perhaps difficult to reconcile with the 'caprice' attributed to them elsewhere (45), but both descriptions suggest a mysterious influence that is hard to understand and to resist. In some of these texts, modern readers will be tempted to see hints, or more, of a materialist determinism that did not really assert itself until well on into the eighteenth century. An example of this tendency is found in no. 44: 'La force et la faiblesse de l'esprit sont mal nommées; elles ne sont, en effet, que la bonne ou la mauvaise disposition des organes du corps'. Even more uncompromising is the assertion that 'Toutes nos passions ne sont autre chose que les divers degrés de la chaleur et de la froideur du sang' (564). Maybe it was the materialist implications of this last maxim that caused it to be discarded in 1666; it hardly leaves room even for *amour-propre,* except as a pure biological drive. Certainly one of the participants in the *sondage* of 1663 was concerned about the compatibility between such statement s and the Christian doctrine of free will and moral responsibility (see *4,* p. 565). The idea of the physical determination of behaviour seems also to be suggested by the theme of unconscious motivation: 'Il s'en faut bien que nous ne connaissions toutes nos volontés' (295). One must however be wary of reading too much *libertin* thought into maxims such as these. Similar statements may be found in the works of Cureau de La Chambre. Perhaps such maxims should simply be classed as 'demystifying statements that discredit conventional knowledge' (*42,* pp. 76-7). Likewise, as we have seen, La Rochefoucauld attributes virtues such as chastity and temperance to physical, or at least to non-moral, causes (1, 17, 205, 566, 593). The theory of the humours, in itself, might appear to modern eyes to embody a materialist doctrine; but the seventeenth-century conception of the soul as a distinct entity was so firm that Descartes's dualism, for instance, as seen in his concept of the 'body-machine', was not regarded for a long time as dangerous to Christian belief. Many Jansenists in particular were also ardent Cartesians.

The Attack on 'Heroic Virtue'

So far we have considered the notion of *vertu,* as undermined by La Rochefoucauld, in its conventional modern sense, reflecting Christian moral values. In seventeenth-century French usage, however, this word (like *générosité*) retained overtones of its Latin connotation, namely 'manliness, manly courage'. The 'pagan virtue' then being attacked by radical Christian moralists was above all the Stoic conception of virtue, *la constance,* heroic fortitude. In 1641, La Mothe le Vayer, a well-known sceptical philosopher, had published a treatise (intended, with Richelieu's blessing, as a counter-blast to rising Jansenism) entitled *De la vertu des païens.* It was a spirited defence of the concept of man's 'natural virtue', and of Stoic philosophy in particular. Its publication had provoked further attacks from Jansenists, in whose eyes no virtue could be genuine unless it was inspired by the love of Christ. This doctrine is central to Jacques Esprit's *La Fausseté des vertus humaines,* and it is in this particular context that many passage of the *Maximes* must be understood, if we are to perceive all the resonances that these texts must have possessed for La Rochefoucauld's first readers. In the frontispiece of 1665, it is Seneca, the foremost representative of Stoic philosophy, who has been unmasked. The assault on Stoicism is very prominent in the early versions of the *Maximes*, notably in the Liancourt manuscript; subsequently La Rochefoucauld gave rather less emphasis to this theme, but he does not neglect it, and his criticisms of the 'heroic ethic' reappear in some of the maxims added in 1678 (e.g. 420, 435, 449, 462, 465, 488).

The whole spectrum of 'heroic virtue', in both the Stoic and the chivalrous traditions, is covered by the 'reductive definition' and other techniques of denigration employed in the *Maximes*. The first relevant 'cluster' of texts (15-26) forms a frontal attack on the virtues proclaimed by the Stoics. 'Cette clémence, dont on fait une vertu, se pratique tantôt par vanité, quelquefois par paresse, souvent par crainte, et presque toujours par tous les trois ensemble' (16; cf. 15). 'Moderation' (i.e. self-restraint in times of good fortune) is likewise said to be inspired by a variety of dubious motives (17, 18). The Stoic virtue *par excellence* is then 'explained' by the familiar reductive process: 'La constance des sages n'est que l'art de renfermer leur agitation dans le cœur' (20). The Stoic claim to regard death with indifference is the target for a final group of maxims in this 'cluster', resulting first in calculated bathos: 'La plupart des hommes meurent parce qu'on ne peut s'empêcher de mourir' (23), and then culminating in the celebrated zeugma: 'Le soleil ni la mort ne se peuvent regarder fixement' (26). Another maxim (24) ends with an eloquent *raccourci* at the expense of the heroic élite: 'à une grande vanité près, les héros sont faits comme les autres hommes.' We have already seen La Rochefoucauld apply his destructive 'dissection technique' to the notion of military valour (215). Later on in the *Maximes*, this criticism of the hero becomes more muted, or at least less frequent; there are even (as we shall see later) some maxims of a more positive kind on this theme. One brief group however (246-8) is quite damning as regards heroic virtue: *générosité*, or its semblance, is nothing but 'une ambition déguisée, qui méprise de petits intérêts, pour aller à de plus grands'; fidelity is merely 'une invention de l'amour-propre, pour attirer la confiance'; and finally, 'la magnanimité méprise tout, pour avoir tout'. What these sham virtues lack, in La Rochefoucauld's eyes, is the essential quality of disinterestedness. Likewise, fidelity in love is worthless if not spontaneous: 'La violence qu'on se fait pour demeurer fidèle à ce qu'on aime ne vaut guère mieux qu'une infidélité' (381). Elsewhere, La Rochefoucauld demands of a hero qualities of intellect and will, not merely physical courage: 'Les grandes âmes ne sont pas celles qui ont moins de passions et plus de vertu que les âmes communes, mais celles qui ont de plus grands desseins' (602), and: 'L'intrépidité doit soutenir le cœur dans les conjurations, au lieu que la seule valeur lui fournit toute la fermeté qui lui est nécessaire dans les périls de la guerre' (614). His approach to the subject of heroism is not merely negative, but certainly sceptical and probing (cf. 219, 220, 221).

It might be asked to what extent La Rochefoucauld admired strength of character as a form of virtue, regardless of the object it is applied to. We have noted the contempt he reserves for 'la faiblesse' (130, 237, 445, etc.) Yet how should we interpret his famous pronouncement: 'Il y a des héros en mal comme en bien' (185)? Is this an approving, 'aesthetic' judgement on grandeur in evil, or an ironic comment on other men's judgements? In the first place, another maxim virtually contradicts it: 'La gloire des grands hommes se doit toujours mesurer aux moyens dont ils se sont servis pour l'acquérir' (157; cf. 190). The irony becomes unmistakable when the same idea is expressed in other terms: 'Il y a des crimes qui deviennent innocents, et même glorieux, par leur éclat, leur nombre et leur excès; de là vient que les voleries publiques sont des habiletés, et que prendre des provinces injustement s'appelle faire des conquêtes' (608). The tone has changed now; this sounds rather like St Augustine's tale of the pirate's retort when Alexander the Great condemned him for his piracy—a story La Rochefoucauld could have gleaned from Jacques Esprit, who incidentally himself uses the expression *héros en mal* (see *7*, p. 1076; *52*, p. 573).

The author's final judgement on Stoicism is found in the extended *réflexion* (504) which formed the conclusion to all the editions of the *Maximes* from 1665 to 1678. This is a tragic meditation on death, or rather on men's futile efforts, throughout the ages, to overcome their fear of death or to avert their eyes from it. Here La Rochefoucauld explicitly places himself in a wholly humanist perspective, excluding all possible Christian consolations (see lines 4-5). He admits that the Stoic virtue of *constance* can at least lend dignity to our dying hour, but as for the philosophers' claims to regard death with indifference, they are quite simply an imposture. 'Je doute', he writes with his customary bluntness, 'que personne de bon sens l'ait jamais cru'. He then goes on to review all the reasoning, all the ruses that men have had recourse to in facing the inevitability of death. So far the author has adopted the neutral tone of the philosopher, but now he begins to shirt his ground. A verb rarely used in the *Maximes* signals this change: 'Il faut éviter de l'envisager [*la mort*] avec toutes ses circonstances, si on ne veut pas croire qu'elle soit le plus grand de tous les maux.' The philosophers, faced with the necessity of dying, tried at least to preserve their reputation for mental courage. Then the sudden intrusion of the first person plural marks the author's final descent from his pedestal into the arena of terrified humanity:

'Contentons-nous, pour faire bonne mine, de ne pas nous dire à nous-mêmes tout ce que nous en pensons, et espérons plus de notre tempérament que de ces faibles raisonnements...' The author's most cogent observation is no doubt the following: 'C'est aussi mal connaître les effets de l'amour-propre que de penser qu'il puisse nous aider à compter pour rien ce qui le doit nécessairement détruire'. There is, inevitably, no conclusion to the debate. The final theme is that of death the great leveller. La Rochefoucauld compares and contrasts the behaviour of 'les grands hommes' and of 'les gens du commun' when faced with their common, implacable enemy.

Great emphasis is therefore placed by La Rochefoucauld on the idea of the contingent nature of man, and no maxim expresses this more fully than the following: 'Toutes nos qualités sont incertaines et douteuses, en bien comme en mal, et elles sont presque toutes à la merci des occasions' (470). Our author's universe is one dominated by the caprices of Fortune, which we have already seen in league with *humeur* as a controlling force in man's existence. The word *fortune* occurs thirty-eight times in the *Maximes*. It controls our daily lives: 'Il faudrait pouvoir répondre de sa fortune, pour pouvoir répondre de ce que l'on fera' (574). In their over-confidence, men do not always acknowledge the role of chance: 'Les gens heureux ne se corrigent guère, et ils croient toujours avoir raison, quand la fortune soutient leur mauvaise conduite' (227). Yet not only the circumstances of our lives, but our individual qualities are governed by its interventions and its revelations: 'La fortune fait paraître nos vertus et nos vices, comme la lumière fait paraître les objets' (380; cf. 1, 323). The men we call heroes are particularly subject to its vicissitudes: 'Quelques grands avantages que la nature donne, ce n'est pas elle seule, mais la fortune avec elle qui fait les héros' (53). Here La Rochefoucauld is probing in an area of great uncertainty. Are men free to control their own destiny? To quite a considerable extent, it seems: 'Il n'y a point d'accidents si malheureux dont les habiles gens ne tirent quelque avantage, ni de si heureux que les imprudents ne puissent tourner à leur préjudice' (59). Yet the very next maxim alters the outlook radically: 'La fortune tourne tout à l'avantage de ceux qu'elle favorise' (60; cf. 58). These contradictory viewpoints can be seen as our author's contribution to a long-standing debate, initiated by Machiavelli, and centred on the question: 'To what extent can human foresight and sagacity (*prudence*) forestall or correct the workings of Fortune, i.e. chance?' On this issue, La Rochefoucauld leans toward pessimism, particularly in a maxim which we have encountered already: 'Il n'y a point d'éloge qu'on ne donne à la prudence; cependant elle ne saurait nous assurer du moindre événement' (65). This is much gloomier than Machiavelli's stated view, that Fortune rules men's affairs one half of the time, but that during the other half, individuals of sufficient *virtù* can do a lot to determine their own fate (*The Prince,* ch. XXV). However, this maxim does not necessarily express our author's final view on the matter, for here is another possibility: 'Il faut gouverner la fortune comme la santé: en jouir quand elle est bonne, prendre patience quand elle est mauvaise, et ne faire jamais de grands remèdes sans un extrême besoin' (392).

Religious Implications

The frequent appearance of themes such as 'Fortune' in a work we have assumed to be a 'demolition of man' in the name of a rigorous Christian doctrine, is but one of several features of the *Maximes* that have led to some profound questioning of the author's motives and beliefs. Many texts appear, as we have seen, to be impregnated with the Augustinian notion of man's incurable corruption. Others, however, do not obviously fit into the pattern, and the work in its final shape gives a distinct impression of 'secularization': the study of behaviour has detached itself from theology, and is being conducted increasingly on purely empirical criteria. The idea of the *Maximes* as a 'school of Christian humility', or as 'preparation for the Gospel's message', comparable in this to Pascal's *Pensées* (5, pp. 16-17), no longer carries a great weight of conviction. Accusations of *libertinage,* from mild indifference to full-blown atheism, have rained down on La Rochefoucauld in recent times. Despite occasional reservations going right back to the 1663 *sondage,* such charges were uncommon until the nineteenth century. By this time, the whole concept of man that presides over our interpretations of literature had changed radically. Let us consider why La Rochefoucauld's credentials as a Christian apologist have so often been questioned. As represented by the Liancourt manuscript, the *Maximes* appear to be a work of unimpeachable orthodoxy, proposing a theocentric interpretation of man's condition. But of the early maxims that refer to God by name, or to a central point of Christian doctrine, only one survived into the later editions (385, devoted to humility, and first published in 1675). For the sake of completeness, one should add that no. 341, likewise introduced in 1675, briefly mentions salvation; and that no. 504 opens with the assurance that the author refers only to 'ce mépris de la mort que les païens se vantent de tirer de leurs propres forces, sans l'espérance d'une meilleure vie'. But that is all. The other explicitly Christian maxims were either eliminated or not published at all. They include such capital statements as: 'Dieu a permis, pour punir l'homme du péché originel, qu'il se fît un dieu de son amour-propre, pour en être tourmenté dans toutes les actions de sa vie' (509; cf. 505, 523, 527, 537, 542, 585, 613). Moreover in the course of his revisions, the author cut out the Christian content in several more (e.g. 9, 65, 170, 202: see *3*, pp. 10, 32, 66-7, 78). Finally, there is no reference at all to religion in the *Réflexions diverses*.

Where, then, should we look for evidence of the author's Christian commitment? Several fairly explicit statements could be cited, but they all lie outside the *Maximes*. The most complete one is in a letter La Rochefoucauld wrote to Le Père Thomas Esprit, on learning about the Dutch pirate edition of his *Maximes*. Associating his own enterprise with that of his correspondent's brother in *La Fausseté des vertus humaines,* he declares: 'l'on n'a pu trop exagérer les misères et les contrariétés du cœur humain pour punir l'orgueil ridicule dont il est rempli, et lui faire voir le besoin qu'il a en toutes choses d'être soutenu et redressé par le christianisme' (*4*, p. 578). Other equally committed statements were put out on the author's behalf. The rather long-winded preface by La Chapelle-Bessé does everything it can to disclose the identity of the author except name him (*4*, p. 269), and it contains several assertions of his Christian purpose. The *Maximes,* we are told, analyse 'le cœur de l'homme corrompu, attaqué de l'orgueil et de l'amour-propre'; in this, the writer is at one with 'bien des auteurs, et même des Pères de l'Église et des saints qui ont pensé que l'amour-propre et l'orgueil étaient l'âme des plus belles actions des païens' (*4*, p. 272; cf. p. 275). Seneca is fiercely criticised in this respect. As for La Rochefoucauld, 'c'est de l'homme abandonné à sa conduite qu'il parle, et non pas du chrétien' (p. 274). The 'Avis au lecteur' refers likewise to the author's 'morale conforme aux pensées de plusieurs Pères de l'Église' (p. 267); and the brief preface which served, with minor modifications, for the 1666, 1671 and 1675 editions describes the author's intentions in a manner similar to La Chapelle-Bessé's (see *4*, pp. 373-7). All these statements are explicit enough, but their authors had an axe to grind, and in any case they must be classed as secondary material.

Some of the arguments used more recently to back up accusations of impiety or religious indifference reveal inadequate acquaintance with seventeenth-century habits of thought. We have already considered the 'materialism' allegedly implicit in La Rochefoucauld's descriptions of the humours and the passions. Similar statements can be found in committed Jansenist writers such as Jacques Esprit, and represent what has been called 'l'extrême pointe poussé par le naturalisme janséniste' (*30*, p. 159). Likewise, La Rochefoucauld's frequent references to Fortune have been seen as anti-Christian. Admittedly, beside the thirty-eight references to this deity, there is only one to God's Providence, and that in a *maxime supprimée*

(613). However, the free juxtaposition of the terms Fortune, Destiny and Providence was common enough at this time, even in the works of some clerical writers, though other theologians and lay moralists attacked this practice as impious (see e.g. *57,* p. 113). Montaigne for instance had defended it in his essay *Des prières* (I, 56). A common assumption seems to have been that 'humour' and 'fortune' still exert influence on this planet, it being the 'sub-lunar' world of the old Aristotelian cosmology—an idea that had not been entirely abandoned.

The most reasonable conclusion to draw from this evidence is probably the one already drawn by Sainte-Beuve in 1840: 'Les *Maximes* de La Rochefoucauld ne contredisent en rien le christianisme, bien qu'elles s'en passent'. Anything more than this moderate view invites an objection: if their author adhered sincerely to Jansenist doctrine, was it not his Christian duty to urge his readers more directly to consider their own salvation? The answer no doubt lies in an aspect of *bienséance,* namely the necessary separation of the sacred and the profane. A lay author with no theological training was expected neither to preach, nor to expound Christian doctrine, of which the sole custodian was the Church. This would be particularly true of an aristocratic 'amateur' addressing an audience of *honnêtes gens.* Corneille had been criticised in the salons for his handling of a religious subject full of tricky theological implications in *Polyeucte.* The effect of this 'taboo' is seen in Mme de La Fayette's novel *La Princesse de Clèves,* in the writing of which La Rochefoucauld may have had a modest part. The heroine is clearly a person of deep piety; her conduct does not really make sense in the absence of this premiss; yet there is no mention of religion, until the final allusion to her last years spent in a convent. The notion of *bienséance* appears to have had a decisive effect here. The questions raised by La Rochefoucauld's enigmatic stance regarding religion are so complex that controversy will never cease, with some eminent authorities confessing to perplexity (e.g. *4,* pp. lxx-lxxi).

The same is true in more general terms about this elusive writer, though whether La Rochefoucauld, or the very form of the maxim, is more to blame is a moot point. Few authors have given a more vivid impression of the complexity and contradictions of man. How many aspects of life are described in the *Maximes* as obscure, difficult to judge, whether it be love (68), human sensibility (80), the techniques of (self-) deception (115), the appearance of straightforwardness (170), the art of growing old (423), or even how to know one's own mind (293), and many more besides! The isolated phenomenon remains unique, being much more apt to elude our grasp than abstract generalities: this applies particularly to humanity (436). The corollary to this is stated elsewhere: 'Pour bien

savoir les choses, il faut en savoir le détail, et comme il est presque
infini, nos connaissances sont toujours superficielles et imparfaites'
(\106). Like Montaigne, La Rochefoucauld offers us an intimation of
the infinite diversity of life, in all its anomalies and inconsistencies;
to such an extent that it may be preferable to speak not of *the*
meaning or interpretation of the *Maximes,* but of their diverse
meanings and interpretations. The difficulty of exegesis is aggravated
by La Rochefoucauld's disconcerting use (comparable in many ways
to Pascal's) of an insufficiently defined, non-technical vocabulary.
When and in what circumstances, for instance, does a virtue that is
systematically denied or reinterpreted continue, or cease, to be a
virtue? (See *15,* pp. 35-6). One feels both the necessity and the near-
impossibility of achieving an adequate synthesis. Transitions are
difficult because one is uncertain of the links (if they exist) between
different facets of La Rochefoucauld's thought. So far we have
looked mainly at the 'negative' sides, dominated by the concepts of
amour-propre and false virtue. Another important group of themes
of the *Maximes* may appear more 'positive' in character, though
never systematically so. It centres above all on the notion of
honnêteté, and it is here that the *Réflexions diverses* come into their
own. The fragmented nature of the maxim form complicates
mightily our attempts at classification; but it can be said in general
that in this other domain, the 'Augustinian' inspiration is largely
replaced by the *mondain* inspiration. It is not always that simple,
however; throughout our reading of the *Maximes* we may find
ourselves uncomfortably placed 'au carrefour de plusieurs morales'
(*29,* p. 40).

Chapter Three

Compensations

The fragmented form of the *Maximes* is not the sole reason for the problems we have encountered. La Rochefoucauld's enthusiasm for the maxim form is clearly bound up with his own mental make-up. Part of him seeks the comforting coherence of Augustinian theology, but another part prefers to envisage reality piecemeal, in its separate compartments and on its different levels. The central antithesis could be said to lie between 'essence' and 'existence', that is between pure intellectual truth and the practice of living. The cleavage is nowhere more apparent than in maxim no. 182. So far we have quoted only its opening simile, but with the whole text the picture changes abruptly: 'Les vices entrent dans la composition des vertus, comme les poisons entrent dans la composition des remèdes: la prudence les assemble et les tempère, et elle s'en sert utilement contre les maux de la vie'. Man's nature may bear the indelible taint of original sin, but it is with such resources as he has that he must perforce organise his life. This is the function of *prudence*. The complete text opens up new perspectives. Although the *Maximes* offer little practical advice on an everyday level, La Rochefoucauld does sometimes consider the requirements of action in the real world: 'On ne doit pas juger du mérite d'un homme par ses grandes qualités, mais par l'usage qu'il en sait faire' (437; cf. 159). His essential moral criteria may depend on purity of intention, but he cannot help noticing that blameworthy motives can produce salutary effects: 'L'intérêt, que l'on accuse de tous nos crimes, mérite souvent d'être loué de nos bonnes actions' (305). This more pragmatic outlook contrasts with that of the 'Augustinian' maxims that loomed so large in the previous chapter. Such changes of viewpoint help to produce the disconcerting ambiguities so often remarked on in the *Maximes*. Various planes of experience are juxtaposed in a manner perplexing to those who seek —as we all do, to some extent—a coherent 'message' in a work that by its very nature refuses to perform such a service.

Quite a number of texts allude to this problem. How difficult it is, we are told, to interpret the world of appearances: 'Il y a des faussetés déguisés qui représentent si bien la vérité, que ce serait mal juger que de ne s'y pas laisser tromper' (282). Elsewhere the same dilemma presents itself on the level of moral judgement: 'Il y a de certains défauts qui, bien mis en œuvre, brillent plus que la vertu même' (354). Here the use of *briller* rather than of *représenter* suggests even more strongly the idea of speciousness; but the problem of distinguishing illusion from reality remains intact. In another maxim, the same problem is evoked in the form of a positive choice: 'Il est difficile de juger si un procédé net, sincère et honnête est un effet de probité ou d'habileté' (170). In all these cases, the ambiguity is located in the deceptive appearances of the world, but sometimes we may suspect that it is artificially created, by the manipulation of language:

> La constance en amour est une inconstance perpétuelle, qui fait que notre cœur s'attache sucessivement à toutes les qualités de la personne que nous aimons, donnant tantôt la préférence à l'une, tantôt à l'autre: de sorte que cette constance n'est qu'une inconstance arrêtée et renfermée dans un même sujet. (175)

However fascinating we may find this maxim, we may still decide that it is essentially a witty quibble. Other maxims create their ambiguity through a genuine juxtaposition, implicit at least, of different points of view. These include one of the most exquisitely moulded of all, impeccable in the perfect balance of its component parts: 'L'espérance, toute trompeuse qu'elle est, sert au moins à nous mener à la fin de la vie par un chemin agréable' (168). Is this a cheerful or a gloomy statement? This must depend on what we expect of life, and of beyond it. Is hope a virtue, or (as Pascal would put it) a *puissance trompeuse*? A virtue, no doubt, from the 'pagan' point of view, given its power of comforting illusion; but there is little trace here of the Christian theological virtue of hope! An even starker confrontation of different planes of experience is found in one of La Rochefoucauld's most celebrated pronouncements on friendship: 'Nous ne pouvons rien aimer que par rapport à nous, et nous ne faisons que suivre notre goût et notre plaisir quand nous préférons nos amis à nous-mêmes; c'est néanmoins par cette préférence seule que l'amitié peut être vraie et parfaite' (81). First, we are told how the world of trusting personal relationships is undermined by the workings of *amour-propre*. The author adds, however, that if our preference for our friends over ourselves were genuinely motivated by Christian love, then the friendship would be 'true' and 'perfect'. In some other cases, the ambiguity of the maxim may concern the nature of the values involved, and the expected tone of disapproval may fade away. This can be perceived, for instance, by comparing three related maxims on the subject of praise, its causes and its effects (these maxims appeared consecutively, in the 1665 edition only):

> On ne blâme le vice et on ne loue la vertu que par intérêt. (597)

> La louange qu'on nous donne sert au moins à nous fixer dans la pratique des vertus. (598)

> L'approbation que l'on donne à l'esprit, à la beauté et à la valeur, les
> augmente, les perfectionne et leur fait faire de plus grands effets qu'ils
> n'auraient été capables de faire d'eux-mêmes. (599)

What in the first case appears to be a blunt condemnation of *amour-propre* then loses its sting when reformulated. A little of that sting is preserved by the 'au moins' of the second text, but the third maxim sounds quite approving: intelligence, beauty and valour merit our praise, which in turn serves to consolidate their good repute. Where is the Jansenist moral stricture here? Is *amour-propre* such a scourge after all?

This kind of ambiguity is associated with the author's love of paradox, and this in its turn can be richly productive of irony. The importance of irony in La Rochefoucauld has not always been recognised (see *30*, pp. 130-46). Some maxims are patently, and some less patently, not intended to be taken in complete earnest. From time to time, the author appears to spring to the defence of the vices he elsewhere condemns. A case in point is jealousy: 'La jalousie est, en quelque manière, juste et raisonnable, puisqu'elle ne tend qu'à conserver un bien qui nous appartient ou que nous croyons nous appartenir, au lieu que l'envie est une fureur qui ne peut souffrir le bien des autres' (28). Here the words *juste* and *raisonnable* can hardly be taken at their face value. Jealousy, which La Rochefoucauld elsewhere describes as 'le plus grand de tous les maux' (503) is exonerated, but only by comparison with another and even uglier vice, which the previous maxim has labelled 'une passion timide et honteuse que l'on n'ose jamais avouer' (27). A similar case involves an unexpected justification of pride: 'Il semble que la nature, qui a si sagement disposé les organes de notre corps pour nous rendre heureux, nous ait aussi donné l'orgueil pour nous épargner la douleur de connaître nos imperfections' (36). Here we have an apparently anti-Augustinian, but possibly tongue-in-the-cheek defence of what Christianity has always regarded as man's fundamental sin, with the aid of a very different philosophical doctrine: naturalism in the tradition of Montaigne, with its unfailing trust in the wisdom of 'Mother Nature'. Another type of irony is unspoken: it results from the reader's own perception of contrasting points of view on a given topic, most obviously when they are concentrated in a single 'cluster' of maxims (e.g. nos. 33-37, all on pride). In the case of isolated texts, the ironical effect will be more dependent on the reader's memory. It may be recalled that the only explicitly Christian maxim to survive in the 1678 edition was on humility, extolled as 'la véritable preuve des vertus chrétiennes' (358). The only other maxim on the same theme in this edition sounded a very different note, for it was an exemplary application of La Rochefoucauld's 'system' to the same notion of humility:

> L'humilité n'est souvent qu'une feinte soumission, dont on se sert pour soumettre les autres: c'est un artifice de l'orgueil qui s'abaisse pour s'élever; et bien qu'il se transforme en mille manières, il n'est jamais mieux déguisé et plus capable de tromper que lorsqu'il se cache sous la figure de l'humilité. (254)

To compare these two texts poses the question whether we can attribute any fixed opinion, or set of opinions, to this chameleon-like writer. In the shorter ironical texts, the effect normally arises from the choice of diction, above all from various forms of repetition. Such patterning can be quite elaborate, as in 'Nous pardonnons souvent à ceux qui nous ennuient, mais nous ne pouvons pardonner à ceux que nous ennuyons' (304). Here we may pause momentarily before perceiving the irony produced by this reversal of our expectations. More often, the 'echo technique' will involve just one or two words, usually paronyms. A fine example of this is found in no. 326: 'Le ridicule déshonore plus que le déshonneur.' What could possibly be more dishonouring than dishonour itself? Such however is the satirical malice of mankind, and such is the importance of prestige, that mockery may indeed provoke more shame than silent disgrace. Sometimes the irony will depend on antithesis within two neatly parallel constructions: 'Nous promettons selon nos espérances, et nous tenons selon nos craintes' (38). Here again we may need a second's pause to grasp the full charge of the irony in the vigorous antithesis / ellipsis (see *57,* pp. 210-11). There is no need to extend the illustrations: La Rochefoucauld has developed these various techniques of irony to a high degree of skill and subtlety.

Such effects as ambiguity and irony suggest a more balanced outlook on the part of the writer than did the rigorous application of a 'system', the limitations of which have now become apparent. In fact we can detect the presence in the *Maximes* of a variety of 'compensation structures', as they have been called (see *50,* pp. 168-85 and *51),* in which form and content achieve a remarkable degree of convergence. The seminal maxim of this type is undoubtedly no. 52: 'Quelque différence qui paraisse entre les fortunes, il y a néanmoins une certaine compensation de biens et de maux qui les rend égales. (This is the only time the word *compensation* is actually used, but the idea it conveys is often present, e.g. in no. 613.) Such maxims are immediately recognisable by their characteristic *quelque ... que* construction. The author's use of this potentially cacophonous form in fact often achieves a fair degree of eloquence and elegance, as in the following examples:

> Quelques grands avantages que la nature donne, ce n'est pas elle seule, mais la fortune avec elle, qui fait les héros. (53)
>
> Quelque éclatante que soit une action, elle ne doit pas passer pour grande, lorsqu'elle n'est pas l'effet d'un grand dessein. (160)
>
> La grâce de la nouveauté et la longue habitude, quelque opposées qu'elles soient, nous empêchent également de sentir les défauts de nos amis. (426; cf. 3, 12, 161, 232, 412, 455, 473, 489, etc.)

Some of the maxims which adopt this structure are firmly optimistic in character, for example: 'Quelque honte que nous ayons méritée, il est presque toujours en notre pouvoir de rétablir notre réputation' (412; cf. 455, 489). Others, built on different rhetorical models, are nevertheless comparable in their theme of 'compensation' and sometimes in their aesthetic effect, such as no. 573: 'On se console souvent d'être malheureux, par un certain plaisir qu'on trouve à le paraître' (cf. 165, 168, 252). Nature, in La Rochefoucauld's world as in La Fontaine's, is seen to achieve some admirable 'compensations' of this kind, and as a form the maxim is admirably suited to expounding this theme.

A central paradox in the moral ideas of La Rochefoucauld is now visible. His deep-rooted pessimism, of mainly theological origin but also produced by the lucidity of a disillusioned mind, never quite succeeds in negating his instinctive belief in the possibilities of human effort, and in the resourcefulness of civilised life. He is rarely as 'cynical' as his reputation would have it, since we often find him judging intentions and actions in terms of moral worth. It is not so much the existence of virtue that he doubts as man's natural inclination towards it, and his capacity to achieve it in its 'pure' form. As Bénichou points out: 'Le sentiment d'inauthenticité qui naît du spectacle de l'homme peut aussi bien s'appeler exigence d'authenticité' (*13*, p. 23). The existence of certain virtues and ideals is clearly stated or implied in a substantial number of maxims. As we saw earlier, the desire for praise can be a powerful stimulus to virtuous deeds: 'Le desir de mériter les louanges qu'on nous donne fortifie notre vertu, et celles que l'on donne à l'esprit, à valeur et à la beauté contribuent à les augmenter' (150). On the other hand, we should be deterred from vice by the fact that evil-doers sometimes receive their just deserts (183). Elsewhere, La Rochefoucauld displays some modest confidence that true values will triumph over false, whenever men are able to see them clearly: 'L'envie est détruite par la véritable amitié, et la coquetterie par le véritable amour' (376). His most enthusiastic pronouncement of this kind was admittedly never published in his lifetime, but that may have been due to the cumbersome expression rather than to the content:

Les philosophes ne condamnent les richesses que par le mauvais usage que nous en faisons; il dépend de nous de les acquérir et de nous en servir sans crime; et au lieu qu'elles nourrissent et accroissent les crimes, comme le bois entretient le feu, nous pouvons les consacrer à toutes les vertus, et les rendre même par là plus agréables et plus éclatantes. (520)

As well as general affirmations of the type just quoted, the *Maximes* also include precise and positive references to particular virtues. Sincerity, the very existence of which appeared undermined by La Rochefoucauld's theory of self-deception, is partly resurrected by this statement: 'La sincérité est une ouverture du cœur. On la trouve en fort peu de gens, et celle que l'on voit d'ordinaire n'est qu'une fine dissimulation, pour attirer la confiance des autres' (62). Once again, the existence of the counterfeit attests the reality, if not the abundance, of the genuine article. Kindness is presented in a similar light: 'Rien n'est plus rare que la véritable bonté: ceux mêmes qui croient en avoir n'ont d'ordinaire que de la complaisance ou de la faiblesse' (481; cf. 365). The existence of gratitude is even more positively affirmed. It may have its limitations and its self-interested aspects, but it does exist, even sometimes to excess: 'Il y a une certaine reconnaissance vive, qui ne nous acquitte pas seulement des bienfaits que nous avons reçus, mais qui fait même que nos amis nous doivent, en leur payant ce que nous leur devons' (438).

True love can also be said to exist, despite our attempts to conceal or disguise it: 'Il n'y a point de déguisement qui puisse longtemps cacher l'amour où il est, ni le feindre où il n'est pas' (70; cf. 68, 74). But it is on the subject of friendship that La Rochefoucauld makes one of his most positive pronouncements (no. 81, quoted above, p. 46). No other maxim states so clearly the paradox of man, torn between the temptations of his sinful condition, and his perception of a moral ideal (*30*, p. 209). Friendship, indeed, much more than love, offers the possibility of defeating *amour-propre* and of achieving something resembling 'pure' virtue. This is clearly because friendship must entail a real preference for one's friend, a real effacement of the self; whereas love, being rooted in sexual desire, necessarily perpetuates the preference of the self for itself.

Such a possibility of 'salvation' remains a little remote, however; the life-line thrown to humanity is tenuous and difficult to grasp. Most of the maxims indicating the author's belief in virtue also contain some intimation of its difficulty, of its rarity. Sometimes a virtue, in its 'pure' state, is so uncommon as to be unknowable and unattainable: 'S'il y a un amour pur et exempt du mélange de nos autres passions, c'est celui qui est caché au fond du cœur, et que nous ignorons nous-mêmes' (69). Even so, love is not the scarcest virtue: 'Quelque rare que soit le véritable amour, il l'est encore moins que la véritable amitié' (473). Yet when these rare qualities manifest themselves, the effect can be almost miraculous: 'L'envie est détruite par la véritable amitié, et la coquetterie par le véritable amour' (376). Far from being a cynic, La Rochefoucauld could be seen, on this evidence, as too demanding an idealist, placing his concept of virtue on too high a pinnacle for average humanity to grasp. As Jean Lafond puts it: 'C'est bien parce que valeurs et essences ont été placées par lui très haut, et peut-être hors de la portée de l'être humain, que La Rochefoucauld ne peut ensuite que déplorer leur absence ici et maintenant' (*34*, p. 721).

As for the other, 'heroic' conception of virtue, we again find a great diversity of judgement in the *Maximes*. A certain choice of texts reveals, as we have seen, the author applying his 'system' to 'la démolition' du héros', to the debunking of 'heroic' virtue. Yet here, too, contrary indications are not hard to find. This upper-crust aristocrat was by no means a 'class deserter' through and through. He does not automatically associate personal merit with noble birth: 'Les grands noms abaissent au lieu d'élever ceux qui ne les savent pas soutenir' (94). But he preserved his belief in aristocratic values, such as disinterestedness and trust: 'Il est plus honteux de se défier de ses amis que d'en être trompé' (84). There is definitely an 'heroic' as well as an 'anti-heroic' current in the *Maximes*. It may be less striking, but it is far from negligible.

As we saw, the assault on Stoicism was a central theme in the earliest maxims, and its importance was enshrined in the frontispiece of 1665. Certain texts however suggest a less systematic hostility to Stoicism, whether it is seen as a general attitude of mind—'Il vaut mieux employer notre esprit à supporter les infortunes qui nous arrivent qu'à prévoir celles qui nous peuvent arriver' (174)—or is expressed in more philosophical terms: 'Nous ne désirerions guère de choses avec ardeur, si nous connaissions parfaitement ce que nous désirons' (439). As regards 'heroic virtue', there are two opposite poles to be distinguished in the *Maximes*. To see this polarity clearly, we have only to compare the most 'positive' and the most 'negative' utterances. To begin with the negative:

> Lorsque les grands hommes se laissent abattre par la longueur de leurs infortunes, ils font voir qu ils ne les soutenaient que par la force de leur ambition, et non par celle de leur âme, et qu'à une grande vanité près, les héros sont faits comme les autres hommes. (24)

This damning statement reveals La Rochefoucauld at his most sceptical —except, of course, that he doesn't claim that great men always behave thus. In contrast, here is his memorable description of what, for the seventeenth century, was the heroic virtue *par excellence:*

> L'intrépidité est une force extraordinaire de l'âme, qui l'élève au-dessus des troubles, des désordres et des émotions que la vue des grands périls pourrait exciter en elle, et c'est par cette force que les héros se maintiennent en un état paisible, et conservent l'usage libre de leur raison dans les accidents les plus surprenants et les plus terribles. (217)

There is no sceptical analysis of motive—only an admiring description of how, in the presence of danger, a man may find enough 'force d'âme' to follow the uncompromising path of 'reason' (cf. the less optimistic nos. 30 and 42). Here and elsewhere we may detect in La Rochefoucauld an instinctive respect for strength of character:

> La même fermeté qui sert à résister à l'amour sert aussi à le rendre violent et durable... (477)

> Il n'y a que les personnes qui ont de la fermeté qui puissent avoir une véritable douceur... (479; cf. 237)

The counterpart to this is an equally firm aversion to mediocrity: 'Les esprits médiocres condamnent d'ordinaire tout ce qui passe à leur portée' (375). But despite these and other similar affirmations (e.g. nos. 185, 387), it is not true, as we saw earlier, that La Rochefoucauld really subscribes to an 'éthique de la force', to any form of 'immoralism' in which aesthetic admiration for strength of will replaces traditional moral criteria. What he repeatedly implies is that 'virtue' is not a natural gift but a conquest, that at the very least it must be willed or chosen (*27*, pp. 352-4).

As for the 'noble' qualities of *générosité* and *magnanimité*, La Rochefoucauld also seems reluctant on occasion to use his familiar 'demolition' tactic to full effect: 'La magnanimité est assez définie par son nom; néanmoins on pourrait dire que c'est le bon sens de l'orgueil, et la voie la plus noble pour recevoir des louanges' (285). The hesitation we may detect in the wording of this maxim may also be found in the remarkable evolution of no. 246, devoted to *générosité*. An early version of this text, found in three manuscripts, reads as follows: 'La générosité, c'est un désir de briller par des actions extraordinaires; c'est un habile et industrieux emploi du désintéressement, de la fermeté en amitié et de la magnanimité, pour aller promptement à une grande réputation' (*3*, p. 99). In its definitive form, however, that of the 1666 edition, the same maxim conforms more visibly to the familiar 'system': 'Ce qui paraît générosité n'est souvent qu'une ambition déguisée, qui méprise de petits intérêts, pour aller à de plus grands'. The impression of increased scepticism goes hand in hand with a notable improvement in form and expression.

Like many of his contemporaries, La Rochefoucauld is eager to
discover to what extent heroes are 'born' according to the laws of
Nature, and to what extent they are 'made' through a timely
intervention of Fortune. It is only on the rare occasions when these
two determining forces—nature and chance, character and
opportunity—are in perfect accord that normal human limitations
can be transcended:

> Quelques grands avantages que la nature donne, ce n'est pas elle seule,
> mais la fortune avec elle qui fait les héros. (53)

> La nature fait le mérite, et la fortune le met en œuvre. (153)

This does not mean, however, that we are but passive agents, bereft
of initiative and responsibility: 'Pour être un grand homme, il faut
savoir profiter de toute sa fortune' (343). This theme is developed
and illustrated in the second longest of the *Réflexions diverses,* no.
XIV, 'Des modèles de la Nature et de la Fortune' (*1,* pp. 130-33).
Nature and Fortune are compared to two painters who pool their
talents and their resources to produce a historical masterpiece. Here
we find a form of idealisation that one might not readily associate
with a sceptic like La Rochefoucauld. In his celebrated double
portrait of Condé and Turenne, which concludes this text, he appears
to have discarded some of his psychological subtlety, and all of his
reputed cynicism, in composing what is above all a *morceau
d'éloquence* (*1,* p. 133). In contrast, the examples incorporated into
the other historical *réflexion* (no. XVII, 'Des événements de ce
siècle') are not devoid of irony: they constitute a review of the most
extraordinary and paradoxical events of the previous half-century,
narrated so as to bring out the idea of man's unpredictable and
precarious existence under the shadow of fickle Fortune. The earlier
text (no. XIV) tends to suggest the opposite idea, namely that history
is shaped above all by the memorable deeds of heroes.

In the final reckoning, La Rochefoucauld does appear to believe
in the hero, in the exceptional individual possessing an ascendancy
which imposes its prestige on less favoured mortals. This is the
quality which, in one of the most eloquent passages of the *Maximes,*
he refers to as *élévation:*

> Il y a une élévation qui ne dépend point de la fortune: c'est un certain air
> qui nous distingue et qui semble nous destiner aux grandes choses; c'est
> un prix que nous nous donnons imperceptiblement à nous-mêmes; c'est
> par cette qualité que nous usurpons les déférences des autres hommes,
> et c'est elle d'ordinaire qui nous met plus au-dessus d'eux que la
> naissance, les dignités, et le mérite même. (399)

The source of this maxim is in the *Oráculo Manual* of Gracián, but in his enthusiasm La Rochefoucauld has made the wording very much his own. We can see this clearly by comparing his text to a mediocre but much more literal translation among the maxims of Mme de Sablé:

> Il y a un certain empire dans la manière de parler et dans les actions, qui se fait faire place partout, et qui gagne par avance la considération et le respect. Il sert en toutes choses, et même pour obtenir ce qu'on demande. (XXVI)

Such enthusiasm is admittedly exceptional in the *Maximes,* for heroic qualities are rare, and La Rochefoucauld more often directs his attention to the prolific race of *les faibles.*

A more positive perspective is therefore emerging. The 'demolition' process, though often conducted with vigour and conviction, does not account for the whole of our author's complex picture of humanity. Even as regards *amour-propre* itself, and its close relations, *intérêt* and *orgueil,* the condemnation admits of many exceptions: 'L'intérêt, qui aveugle les uns, fait la lumière des autres' (40). Pride enables us to turn a blind eye to our imperfections (36); self-interest causes less dereliction of duty than does boredom (172), and can often be the source of *bonnes actions* (305). These observations apply to personal relationships some of the 'mechanisms of compensation' that we have already studied. Although he wrote that self-interest can make rulers seek affection from their subjects (15), La Rochefoucauld does not extend the functioning of *amour-propre* into the collective, political realm, unlike Pascal, who noted that 'On a tiré de la concupiscence des règles admirables de police, de morale et de justice', and that this fact in itself proves 'la grandeur de l'homme' (*Pensées,* ed. Lafuma, 211, 106). The only important general statement in the *Maximes* about the positive collective uses of *amour-propre* occurs, as we have seen, in the second half of no. 182. Here the function of *prudence* is compared to that of the apothecary measuring out and mixing in harmful ingredients, in order to produce healing medicines—or, in more abstract terms, using man's very imperfections to protect him against the ills of an imperfect world. The good which is thus extracted from evil is only a relative good, a mere substitute for the true Good; but it at least enables men to direct their common self-interest towards creating a tolerable existence for themselves (see 5, pp. 21-2; *30,* pp. 147-9).

These lines in praise of human resourcefulness nevertheless remain an isolated text in the *Maximes,* and are virtually cancelled out by the equally important and familiar maxim no. 65, according to which 'la prudence [...] ne saurait nous assurer du moindre événement'. Nevertheless these two texts, plus one or two others, have inspired a bold reinterpretation of La Rochefoucauld's thought by Louis Hippeau (*25*), according to whom the author's Jansenist allegiance was simply a smoke-screen to hide his true convictions, which were Epicurean. Being an atheist, materialist doctrine, Epicureanism was highly suspect at this time, and one can well imagine its seventeenth-century adepts observing a certain discretion; but to use Jansenism as camouflage would not have made much sense, for at this very moment in time, the inhabitants of Port-Royal were being persecuted with a *Formulaire,* in signing which they had to condemn as heretical five propositions allegedly extracted from the *Augustinus.* Augustinism and Epicureanism did however have an important common feature: the belief in *amour-propre,* that is in the search for individual pleasure and profit, as the guiding motive of human behaviour. In fact, Hippeau's case rests not so much on any text by La Rochefoucauld as on a letter published two years after his death by the chevalier de Méré, the celebrated salon *moraliste* and self-styled *professeur d'honnêteté,* recounting a conversation he claims to have had with the author of the *Maximes*. La Rochefoucauld is made to utter a number of paradoxical statements in praise of Epicurus, culminating in the celebrated remark that 'dans la morale, Sénèque était un hypocrite et [...] Épicure était un saint' (*4*, p. 593). The reliability of Méré as witness in these matters is difficult to assess, but given that his reputation for seriousness was less than impeccable, most biographers and critics have remained very sceptical about La Rochefoucauld's alleged Epicureanism (see e.g. *30*, pp. 96-100).

What is undeniable, however, is that in the years following the death of our author, the 'Epicurean' interpretation of *amour-propre* made remarkable progress. Already in 1672, Nicole in his *Essais de morale* describes it as 'la source et le fondement de tout le commerce qui se pratique entre les hommes'; and in the same year as the 'definitive' edition of the *Maximes,* the 'rival' volume by Mme de Sablé and the abbé d'Ailly contained the following thoughts on the matter:

> Quoique par ce principe il soit vrai de dire que les hommes n'agissent jamais sans intérêt, on ne doit pas croire pour cela que tout soit corrompu, qu'il n'y ait ni justice, ni probité dans le monde. Il y a des gens qui se conduisent par des intérêts honnêtes et louables. C'est ce juste discernement de l'amour-propre bien réglé, quoique rapportant toutes choses à soi-même, mais dans toute l'étendue des lois de la société civile, qui fait ce qu'on appelle honnêtes gens dans le monde. (Ailly, maxim 3, in *7*, p. 262)

L'amour-propre bien réglé—the expression is worth noting. So is the link established between it and the notion of *honnêteté*. This 'Epicurean' view of self-interest was in fact to become a major source of eighteenth-century utilitarianism, enshrined in particular in two famous texts. Mandeville's *Fable of the Bees,* a satirical poem published in 1705, popularised the idea of 'vices privés, source de bienfaits publics' (see *49*). Helvétius's *De l'esprit* (1758) offered a new description of *amour-propre* as 'un sentiment gravé en nous par la nature'—for the benefit, obviously, of the entire human race. Jeremy Bentham, in his *Introduction to the Principles of Morals and Legislation* (1789) associated the 'unjustly maligned trio', La Rochefoucauld, Mandeville and Helvétius, in a hymn of praise. So far as the first of them was concerned, this was a misinterpretation; yet the *Maximes,* as we have seen, are not without their rays of hope. Indeed, this work, far from being obsessively monothematic—an impression that can only be given by carefully selecting the 'Augustinian' texts—offers an undeniable variety of subject-matter, and also of implied philosophical attitudes, some of which may not appear basically compatible. The explanation of this puzzling feature —aggravated, obviously, by the fragmentation of the *Maximes*—lies largely in the nature of the public for which La Rochefoucauld was writing. He intended his *recueil* as instructive entertainment for the varied public that constituted Mme de Sablé's circle. More widely, it was the salons in general that provided a reading public of 'above-average *honnêtes gens*' for works such as the *Maximes*. As Louis van Delft puts it: 'La réflexion des moralistes dut pour une bonne part sa fortune à l'émergence d'un nouveau type de culture' (*17*, pp. 151-6). The new public, nurtured in the salons, did not consist to any great extent of men of learning, but rather of intelligent individuals of both sexes, averagely educated, whose wits had been sharpened by constant discussion of abstract topics concerning social relationships. They were capable of demonstrating their *esprit de finesse* in areas of subtlety such as *l'honnêteté, le goût* and *le je ne sais quoi*. It was a common sensitivity and a shared standard of taste that brought them together.

The 'society games' and 'social entertainment' ingredient of the *Maximes* is evident throughout, but most of all in the texts added in the last three editions published by the author (i.e. nos. 301-504). Some of the perennial themes of society conversation are well represented, for instance, in the following maxims:

> Il est du véritable amour comme de l'apparition des esprits: tout le monde en parle, mais peu de gens l'ont vu. (76)

> L'amour prête son nom à un nombre infini de commerces qu'on lui attribue, et où il n'a non plus de part que le Doge à ce qui se fait à Venise. (77)
>
> Le plus grand miracle de l'amour, c'est de guérir de la coquetterie. (349)
>
> Les vieux fous sont plus fous que les jeunes. (444)
>
> Il ne sert à rien d'être jeune sans être belle, ni d'être belle sans être jeune. (497)

Women in love, the amorous foibles of old age, the doubtful sanity of the elderly—three recurrent topics, typical of light-hearted, almost frivolous, society conversation. Even some maxims that could *à la rigueur* be classified as 'Augustinian' are formulated so as to produce a provocative effect, particularly in mixed company. Such maximes include: 'La plupart des femmes ne pleurent pas la mort de leurs amants pour les avoir aimés, mais pour paraître plus dignes d'être aimées' (362) or even: 'L'éducation que l'on donne d'ordinaire aux jeunes gens est un second amour-propre qu'on leur inspire' (261). The art of paradox, as perfected in the *Maximes,* is designed to stimulate lively contestation in any group of like-minded *gens du monde* (see *16,* pp. 417-20). La Rochefoucauld was earnest in his condemnation of *amour-propre,* but he also saw a certain 'entertainment value' in the provocative nature of this theme: its usual effect is to make us spring to our own defence, and also (since the causes are inseparable) to that of our fellow accused. In all this banter a certain *esprit du jeu* is at large, and linguistic games and society games are closely related (see *42,* pp. 112-15). The alliance of theology and *mondanité* which we find in the *Maximes* may seem rather forced and precarious to us, but so far as we can tell it was quite typical of the company that sometimes gathered in Mme de Sablé's fashionable apartment within the walls of Port-Royal de Paris. The texts which most loudly contradict the *mondain* tone are now to be found among the *maximes écartées* or the *maximes supprimées* (e.g. 509, 511, 520, 523, 527, 537, 564, 568, 589, 613). This may well have been the reason for their relegation.

One of the foremost French accomplishments, in the seventeenth century and since, has been the art of refined conversation. Although La Rochefoucauld does not devote a large amount of space to this topic, what he has to say about it is quite noteworthy. Several maxims describe the manner in which *amour-propre* undermines the basic precondition of civilised conversation, which is that we should take at least as much interest in the person we are talking to as in ourselves. To this recommendation, *amour-propre,* almost by definition, is flatly opposed. Sometimes La Rochefoucauld puts this point briefly and pungently:

On parle peu, quand la vanité ne fait pas parler. (137)

On aime mieux dire du mal de soi-même que de n'en point parler. (138)

Ce qui fait que les amants et les maîtresses ne s'ennuient point d'être ensemble, c'est qu'ils parlent toujours d'eux-mêmes. (312; cf. 313, 314, 364, 383)

Elsewhere he examines this problem in greater detail, in a brief *réflexion*. He presents a dramatic caricature of the selfish obsessions that ruin conversation, in a text we have already examined (see above, no. 510, quoted on p. 28). A more thoughtful and sober analysis is to be found in no. 139:

Une des choses qui font que l'on trouve si peu de gens qui paraissent raisonnables et agréables dans la conversation, c'est qu'il n'y a presque personne qui ne pense plutôt à ce qu'il veut dire qu'à répondre précisément à ce que l'on lui dit. Les plus habiles et les plus complaisants se contentent de montrer seulement une mine attentive, au même temps que l'on voit, dans leurs yeux, et dans leur esprit, un égarement pour ce qu'on leur dit, et une précipitation pour retourner à ce qu'ils veulent dire, au lieu de considérer que c'est un mauvais moyen de plaire aux autres, ou de les persuader, que de chercher si fort à plaire à soi-même, et que bien écouter et bien répondre est une des plus grandes perfections qu'on puisse avoir dans la conversation.

An almost identical text appears as no. 31 of the *Maximes* of Mme de Sablé. It may therefore be a passage on which they had collaborated, but given that the half-dozen variants in Mme de Sablé's version are stylistically so inferior, it seems more likely that it originated from her. This same theme—which could be summed up as the need for politeness in conversation (see *45*, pp. 58-9)—is further developed in no. IV of the *Réflexions diverses,* entitled simply 'De la conversation':

Ce qui fait que si peu de personnes sont agréables dans la conversation, c'est que chacun songe plus à ce qu'il veut dire qu'à ce que les autres disent. Il faut écouter ceux qui parlent, si on en veut être écouté; il faut leur laisser la liberté de se faire entendre, et même de dire des choses inutiles. Au lieu de les contredire ou de les interrompre, comme on fait souvent, on doit, au contraire, entrer dans leur esprit et dans leur goût, montrer qu'on les entend, leur parler de ce qui les touche, louer ce qu'ils disent autant qu'il mérite d'être loué, et faire voir que c'est plutôt par choix qu'on les loue que par complaisance. (*I*, pp. 116-17)

The first rule of conversation is therefore to pay at least as much attention to the personality of the individual one is addressing, as to the ideas or feelings one is trying to express. Clearly La Rochefoucauld regards conversation not just as an exchange of ideas, nor even as a social ritual, but in the first place as an opportunity to develop, or ruin, a personal relationship. He also sees it as an occasion when delicate feelings are liable to be hurt by thoughtless remarks. Some of his advice suggests a high degree of sensitivity on the interlocutor's part: 'Il faut éviter de contester sur des choses indifférentes, faire rarement des questions, qui sont presque toujours inutiles' (ibid., p. 117). Banning the interrogative seems a rather drastic step! What strikes the reader most forcibly in this earnest discussion of social etiquette is the tacit assumption that, given the right degree of sensitive awareness, it *is* possible for men to overcome the aggressive effects of their *amour-propre,* in the interests of social harmony. To do this is indeed the first duty imposed by the code of *honnêteté.* It is often assumed in the *Réflexions diverses* that some individuals at least can withstand those temptations of egoism so often treated as irresistible in the *Maximes.*

As for that other ingredient of refined conversation, *l'esprit* (in the sense of 'wit'), there is little that is explicit to be gleaned from La Rochefoucauld, except of course in the formulation of so many maxims that offer examples of seventeenth-century wit at its best. It is not easy to fix the exact connotation of the word every time it is used in the *Maximes.* As a faculty of perception, *l'esprit* is somewhat belittled by La Rochefoucauld, in comparison with that more intuitive mode of awareness which he calls *le cœur* or *l'âme* (see nos. 43, 80, 98, 102, 108). The *Maximes* also offer a few conventional salon definitions of related qualities, such as: 'La politesse de l'esprit consiste à penser des choses honnêtes et délicates' (99), or: 'La galanterie de l'esprit est de dire des choses flatteuses d'une manière agréable' (100). Where the subtlety really comes into its own is in La Rochefoucauld's rejection of the time-honoured distinction between *esprit* and *jugement:*

> On s'est trompé lorsqu'on a cru que l'esprit et le jugement étaient deux choses différentes: le jugement n'est que la grandeur de la lumière de l'esprit; cette lumière pénètre le fond des choses, elle y remarque tout ce qu'il faut remarquer, et aperçoit celles qui semblent imperceptibles. Ainsi il faut demeurer d'accord que c'est l'étendue de la lumière de l'esprit qui produit tous les effets qu'on attribue au jugement. (97)

However, La Rochefoucauld's masterpiece of fine psychological tuning, of the kind we associate with the best seventeenth-century *préciosité,* is to be found in the sixteenth of the *Réflexions diverses,* 'De la différence des esprits' (*1,* 135-40). It consists of a long series of attempted distinctions, some fifteen in all, between different kinds of 'wit', such as *grand esprit, bel esprit, bon esprit,* and *esprit de finesse*—the latter being a markedly different concept in La Rochefoucauld and in Pascal—and other related concepts. There is a certain element of gratuitousness about these distinctions which reappears in some other texts in the *Réflexions diverses,* and notably in no. X, 'Du goût'. 'De la différence des esprits' is an imitation, but by no means a slavish one, of an immensely popular treatise on 'scholastic' psychological classification by the Spanish writer Juan Huarte, three times translated into French under the title *L'Examen des esprits* (see *16,* pp. 421-2).

The principal echoes of salon conversation to be found in the *Maximes* are naturally contained in the scores of maxims devoted to the theme of love. Quite a few of them would have served well as answers to the *Questions d'amour* which were so popular in a number of salons (see above, p. 12), including Mme de Sablé's circle, for the 'Portefeuilles Vallant' contain a collection of thirty-two such questions which have been attributed to the marquis de Sourdis (see *26,* pp. 138-9). A number of maxims raise questions which are discussed in the novels of Mlle de Scudéry (see *28,* pp. 107-109), for example the distinction between jealousy and envy made in no. 28, or the opposition between *les qualités de l'âme* and *les qualités de l'esprit,* as in no. 80; what is the best punishment for infidelity, and when a lover may reasonably be jealous (359, 360). Some of La Rochefoucauld's evocations of *le véritable amour* no doubt allude to the *précieux* doctrines of love expounded in these same novels, and subsequently in many salons (e.g. nos. 76, 349, 376, 402). Elsewhere we encounter the equally *précieux* theme of the incompatibility of love and marriage (113, 364, 547). Some of the more memorable similes and metaphors that La Rochefoucauld has contributed to the literature of love are but brilliant variations on themes already current in the salons of his day, for example:

> Il n'y a qu'une sorte d'amour, mais il y en a mille différentes copies. (74)

> L'amour, aussi bien que le feu, ne peut subsister sans un mouvement continuel, et il cesse de vivre dès qu'il cesse d'espérer ou de craindre. (75; cf. 76, 77)

> La plus juste comparaison qu'on puisse faire de l'amour, c'est celle de la fièvre; nous n'avons non plus de pouvoir sur l'un que sur l'autre, soit pour sa violence, ou pour sa durée. (638)

Only one or two of these comparisons strike one as possibly original, for instance: 'La grâce de la nouveauté est à l'amour ce que la fleur est sur les fruits: elle y donne un lustre qui s'efface aisément, et qui ne revient jamais' (274). It is the bitter-sweet flavour of this last simile that gives it the authentic stamp of La Rochefoucauld, who could often be indulgent towards the emotion of love, as in this final sentence from the twelfth of the *Réflexions diverses:* 'L'amour, lui seul, a fait plus de maux que tout le reste ensemble, et personne ne doit entreprendre de les exprimer; mais comme il fait aussi les plus grands biens de la vie, au lieu de médire de lui, on doit se taire: on doit le craindre et le respecter toujours' (*1*, p. 128).

Despite the frivolity and the caustic wit that we discover in the maxims devoted to love, the lurking presence of *amour-propre* (e.g. in 262, 324) ensures that a more sombre note will often be struck. This is particularly true of the handling of the theme of jealousy, which as we saw is described as 'le plus grand de tous les maux' (503). Jealousy is not only a painful emotion, but a shaming and demeaning one (446; cf. 443). How much would we sacrifice in order to be spared it! (395) Occasionally the sheer force of intense love can keep jealousy at bay (336), but once established it cannot easily be dislodged: 'La jalousie naît toujours avec l'amour, mais elle ne meurt pas toujours avec lui' (361). Elsewhere our author, with a kind of sombre fascination, dwells upon its paradoxes (472). One of the *Réflexions diverses* is entitled 'De l'incertitude de la jalousie' (VIII; *1*, p. 123). It is precisely these shifting sands, the constantly changing perspectives of the jealous imagination, that form the real source of the lover's torture: 'On croit tout, et on doute de tout; on a de la honte et du dépit d'avoir cru et d'avoir douté; on se travaille incessamment pour arrêter son opinion, et on ne la conduit jamais à un lieu fixe'. La Rochefoucauld's analysis of jealousy stands at the fountain-head of a long tradition—that of the French psychological novel, beginning with Mme de La Fayette and culminating in Proust, whose treatment of this theme provides some striking illustrations of the viewpoints expressed in the *Maximes*. In both authors, love and *amour-propre* are presented as an inexhaustible source of paradoxes.

One aspect of the *Maximes* that may cause today's readers some perplexity, not to say irritation or worse, lies in the many apparently cruel, or at least flippant, remarks about women. In his self-portrait, La Rochefoucauld declares: 'J'ai une civilité fort exacte parmi les femmes, et je ne crois pas avoir jamais rien dit devant elles qui leur ait pu faire de la peine' (*4*, p. 257). He may have said nothing in their presence, but what he wrote behind their back bears few traces of such civility! On perusing the *Maximes,* we come across such choice comments as:

> Le moindre défaut des femmes qui se sont abandonnées à faire l'amour, c'est de faire l'amour. (131)

> Il y a peu d'honnêtes femmes qui ne soient pas lasses de leur métier. (361)

> La plupart des honnêtes femmes sont des trésors cachés, qui ne sont en sûreté que parce qu'on ne les cherche pas. (368: cf. 241, 474, 552)

The majority of these quips first appeared in one of the later editions of the *Maximes* (1671, 1675 or 1678); and it was in 1675 that the author added a sentence to the very first maxim, thus setting as it were the tone for the whole work: '... et ce n'est pas toujours par valeur et par chasteté que les hommes sont vaillants et que les femmes sont chastes'. Thus, far from regretting such 'lapses', La Rochefoucauld compounded them progressively. However we must remember that it is only in the very recent past that the attitudes embodied in such pleasantries have become generally taboo. They were the stock-in-trade of boulevard comedy until well on into the present century, and their echoes can still be heard on the screen, large and small, today. In the seventeenth century, they were part of an ongoing 'querelle des femmes' which opposed 'l'esprit gaulois' and 'l'esprit courtois', a controversy which had been very much alive since the Middle Ages. It is only in such a context that a play like Molière's *L'École des femmes* can be fully understood. In his scandalous collection of largely authentic tales, the *Histoire amoureuse des Gaules,* the most celebrated author of *maximes d'amour,* Bussy-Rabutin, showed himself even more insensitive (as today's eyes would see it) towards women than La Rochefoucauld had ever been. What we need above all, in order to judge such matters, is an accurate historical perspective, and this is not always easy to acquire.

The Concept of *honnêteté*

Where, then, does the path of wisdom lie? We would hardly expect a writer such as La Rochefoucauld, having so firmly proclaimed the universality of *amour-propre,* to announce with his next breath that he has found a panacea for all mankind's moral ills. This is even less likely since humanity has not only its incurable egoism to contend with, but another propensity as well, that our author refers to as its *folie.* Like *amour-propre* but to a lesser extent, *la folie* is seen as the rule rather than the exception among men: 'La folie nous suit dans tous les temps de la vie. Si quelqu'un paraît sage, c'est seulement parce que ses folies sont proportionnées à son âge et à sa fortune' (207). Although it appears in only a handful of maxims, this theme has its importance: it places La Rochefoucauld firmly beside Montaigne in the mainstream tradition of French humanism, the fountain-head of which was Erasmus's *In Praise of Folly.* For the supreme paradox is that such 'folly' forms part of true wisdom, as we all learn in good time: 'En vieillissant, on devient plus fou et plus sage' (210). This is a rule from which none of us is exempt: 'Qui vit sans folie n'est pas si sage qu'il croit' (209), and as a consequence,

'C'est une grande folie de vouloir être sage tout seul' (231). La
Rochefoucauld leaves us to decide exactly what this 'folie' consists
of. Mme de Sévigné asked that very question in a letter of February
1672: 'Hélas! le moyen de vivre sans folie, c'est-à-dire sans fantaisie?
et un homme n'est-il pas fol, qui croit être sage en ne s'amusant et en
ne se divertissant de rien?' (quoted in 4, p. 53, n. 1). Some weeks
later, she added a further gloss by surmising that La Rochefoucauld
had intended to 'louer les fantaisies, c'est-à-dire les passions', and in
her next letter to Mme de Grignan, she confirms, having presumably
consulted the author in the meantime, that the intention of the maxim
was indeed anti-stoic. La Rochefoucauld also suggests that 'folly' can
form part of our practical resourcefulness: 'Il arrive quelquefois des
accidents dans la vie où il faut être un peu fou pour se bien tirer'
(310). 'Folly' is certainly a factor in our mental make-up that he
does not intend us to ignore.

If 'folly' is seen as necessary for survival, that is because survival
is indeed the aim: La Rochefoucauld aspires to make life as liveable
as possible, given mankind's severe limitations. This is bound up
with the notion of *honnêteté* which emerges from some key texts in
the *Maximes* and above all in the *Réflexions diverses*. These define a
more modest aspiration than the heroic values that our author most
often rejects; but it can be a demanding ideal nevertheless. The terms
honnête homme and *honnêteté*, in the elegant usage of the time, were
often ambiguous to the extent that they embodied both a moral and a
social ideal: an *honnête homme* could be an *homme de bien,*
irreproachable from the ethical point of view, and/or a 'good
mixer', a 'social success' whose demeanour produces perfect
acceptability in all the 'best circles'. The two explicit definitions of
this term offered in the *Maximes* lay stress on each aspect in turn.
Firstly, on the moral dimension: 'Les faux honnêtes gens sont ceux
qui déguisent leurs défauts aux autres et à eux-mêmes; les vrais
honnêtes gens sont ceux qui les connaissent parfaitement, et les
confessent' (202). Here self-knowledge is obviously as important as
moral uprightness. The second definition, however, without
excluding moral considerations, is more suggestive of socially
acceptable behaviour: 'Le vrai honnête homme est celui qui ne se
pique de rien' (203). This same idea is expressed in identical terms—
perhaps in a conscious borrowing—by the self-appointed authority in
these matters, Méré. His ideal is to 'exceller en tout ce qui sied bien
aux honnêtes gens, sans néanmoins se piquer de rien' (quoted in 4,
pp. 51-2; 6, p. 111). *Se piquer* commonly meant 'to take pride' and
hence 'to make a show of', 'to give oneself airs'; its use here in the
negative suggests absence of pretentiousness, and hence an *amour-
propre* under firm control. The first of these two maxims also
suggests a certain transparency: the perfect *honnête homme* has

absolutely nothing to hide. This notion is confirmed by no. 206: 'C'est être véritablement honnête homme que de vouloir être toujours exposé à la vue des honnêtes gens'.

The true nature of *honnêteté,* according to La Rochefoucauld, is revealed when seen against the background of his concept of *amour-propre.* As we read at the beginning of the 'grand portrait', this universal impulse, if left unchecked, 'rend les hommes idolâtres d'eux-mêmes, et les rendrait les tyrans des autres, si la fortune leur en donnait les moyens'. So if human society is not to degenerate into perpetual conflict, we must learn to live with this egoism, our own and above all that of others. In the words of Mitton, a seventeenth-century *libertin* and wit: 'C'est ce ménagement de bonheur pour nous et pour les autres que l'on doit appeler l'honnêteté, qui n'est à le bien prendre que l'amour-propre bien ménagé' (see *6,* p. 36). This last phrase recalls l'abbé d'Ailly's formula, *l'amour-propre bien réglé* (see above, p. 55).. La Rochefoucauld himself could have offered no better definition. *Honnêteté* involves a kind of tacit pact, a *modus vivendi,* an acceptance of 'la comédie humaine' and all that it entails, together with a commitment to build a tolerable social order on the basis of this recognition. This could be seen as a more practical and optimistic interpretation than we proposed earlier of maxim no. 87: 'Les hommes ne vivraient pas longtemps en société, s'ils n'étaient les dupes les uns des autres'. The victims of illusion are now seen as willing dupes, resigned to life's inadequacies and frustrations: 'Le sage trouve mieux son compte à ne point s'engager qu'à vaincre' (549; cf. *13,* pp. 31-7; *42,* pp. 107-111). It is in the second of his *Réflexions diverses* that La Rochefoucauld discusses this question most comprehensively. He stresses above all the need for tact and self-restraint in our relationships with others, even for a certain kind of dissimulation:

> Chacun veut trouver son plaisir et ses avantages aux dépens des autres; on se préfère toujours à ceux avec qui on se propose de vivre, et on leur fait presque toujours sentir cette préférence; c'est ce qui trouble et qui détruit la société. Il faudrait du moins savoir cacher cette préférence, puisqu'il est trop naturel en nous pour nous en pouvoir défaire; il faudrait faire son plaisir de celui des autres, ménager leur amour-propre, et ne le blesser jamais. (*1,* p. 112)

This *réflexion* is really an essay on the conditions of mutual compatibility and tolerance in civilised society. Here we do not find La Rochefoucauld denouncing the social comedy, but going a long way towards accepting it. We have to make concessions all the time, he declares, but we must never do so to the point where we begin to forfeit our own authenticity:

Il faut contribuer, autant qu'on le peut, au divertissement des personnes avec qui on veut vivre; mais il ne faut pas être toujours chargé du soin d'y contribuer. La complaisance est nécessaire dans la société, mais elle doit avoir des bornes: elle devient une servitude quand elle est excessive; il faut du moins qu'elle paraisse libre, et qu'en suivant le sentiment de nos amis, ils soient persuadés que c'est le nôtre aussi que nous suivons. (*1*, p. 113)

Discretion and tact form part of the art of conversation: they produce a sympathetic openness which always stops short of intrusion into the other person's private domain:

On doit aller au-devant de ce qui peut plaire à ses amis, chercher les moyens de leur être utile, leur épargner des chagrins, leur faire voir qu'on les partage avec eux quand on ne peut les détourner, les effacer insensiblement sans prétendre de les arracher tout d'un coup, et mettre en la place des objets agréables, ou du moins qui les occupent. On peut leur parler des choses qui les regardent, mais ce n'est qu'autant qu'ils le permettent, et on y doit garder beaucoup de mesure: il y a de la politesse, et quelquefois même de l'humanité, à ne pas entrer trop avant dans les replis de leur cœur; ils ont souvent de la peine à laisser voir tout ce qu'ils en connaissent, et ils en ont encore davantage quand on pénètre ce qu'ils ne connaissent pas. (*1*, p. 114)

This and other passages of the *Réflexions* bear witness to a delicacy of feeling on the author's part, which some of his better-known and more 'cynical' utterances might not lead us to suspect. Above all, the implication behind these exhortations—as frequent here as they are uncommon in the *Maximes*—is that men are generally capable, if they make the effort, of exercising enough control over the anarchic forces of *amour-propre* to make civilised relationships possible, and even enjoyable. It no longer seems to be axiomatic that 'L'amour-propre est plus habile que le plus habile homme du monde' (4). In several of the *Réflexions,* man is credited with genuine moral discernment—with enough of it, at least, to achieve a worthwhile degree of self-knowledge and to counteract the destructive effects of *amour-propre* in determining his own actions. *L'honnêteté,* according to La Rochefoucauld, has been seen as a code of behaviour founded on purely aesthetic criteria, and pursued as a substitute for an unattainable moral ideal (see *55*); but there is a difference between affirming, as he often does, that moral values cannot be achieved by men in their 'pure' state, and that man is radically incapable of any morally valid action. Nor is the kind of dissimulation we have just seen our author recommending a further sign of man's corruption; it is more like that everyday, watered-down form of charity that we call discretion or considerateness, or simply tact (see *27*, pp. 355-9; *30*, pp. 101-105). Like other moralists writing within the orbit of Port-Royal, such as Nicole, La

Rochefoucauld often admits of a certain compromise between
Jansenist intransigence and more worldly values, in the interest of
practical living.

Nevertheless an element of aesthetic judgement is definitely
present in La Rochefoucauld's concept of *honnêteté*. His first
requirement of the *honnête homme* is a kind of 'personal
authenticity' that in its basic form is simply an ability to be one's
own spontaneous, natural self—but how difficult had the social
hierarchy and the artificial culture of the salons made such an
achievement! This problem forms the nub of the third of the
Réflexions diverses, entitled 'De l'air et des manières':

> Ce qui fait que la plupart des petits enfants plaisent, c'est qu'ils sont
> encore renfermés dans cet air et dans ces manières que la nature leur a
> donnés, et qu'ils n'en connaissent point d'autres. Ils les changent et
> corrompent quand ils sortent de l'enfance: ils croient qu'il faut imiter ce
> qu'ils voient faire aux autres, et ils ne le peuvent parfaitement imiter; il y
> a toujours quelque chose de faux et d'incertain dans toute imitation. Ils
> n'ont rien de fixe dans leurs manières ni dans leurs sentiments; au lieu
> d'être en effet ce qu'ils veulent paraître, ils cherchent à paraître ce qu'ils
> ne sont pas. Chacun veut être un autre, et n'être plus ce qu'il est: ils
> cherchent une contenance hors d'eux-mêmes, et un autre esprit que le
> leur; ils prennent des tons et des manières au hasard; ils en font
> l'expérience sur eux, sans considérer que ce qui convient à quelques-
> uns ne convient pas à tout le monde, qu'il n'y a point de règle générale
> pour les tons et pour les manières, et qu'il n'y a point de bonnes copies.
> (*1*, p. 115)

However, despite the long reference to the child's spontaneity, La
Rochefoucauld implies elsewhere that the achievement of such
'naturalness' involves an element of art. This is true even of the
direct expression of feeling: to each emotion corresponds a specific
tone of voice, it requires a particular gesture and facial expression.
The wrong choice of tone or gesture will suffice to make an
individual appear unconvincing and unattractive: 'Tous les sentiments
ont chacun un ton de voix, des gestes et des mines qui leur sont
propres, et ce rapport, bon ou mauvais, agréable ou désagréable, est
ce qui fait que les personnes plaisent ou déplaisent' (255). It has been
pointed out that this concept of 'appropriateness' implies the same
stylisation of gestures and attitudes as is required of a good actor.
This observation is confirmed by the earlier, manuscript version of
the same text, which included the words: 'c'est ce qui fait les bons et
les mauvais comédiens' (see *3*, pp. 103-104; *47*, pp. 71-2). This is
true of all conduct, in that the spontaneous promptings of *amour-
propre* must be 'overlaid'—since they can never be entirely
suppressed—by a more reflective kind of calculation, based on
aesthetic and hedonist considerations as much as on moral judgement,
if not more. La Rochefoucauld repeatedly stresses the subtlety and

the elusiveness of the criteria involved, which are intuitive rather than rational: 'On peut dire de l'agrément, séparé de la beauté, que c'est une symétrie dont on ne sait point les règles, et un rapport secret des traits ensemble, et des traits avec les couleurs, et avec l'air de la personne' (240). The first of the *Réflexions,* 'Du vrai' equates beauty and truth in that both are absolutes, not to be judged in their 'pure' state by any comparative considerations. This idea is illustrated by means of a parallel between the grandiose Château de Chantilly, seat of the Condé family, and a more modest town residence familar to our author, the Hôtel de Liancourt:

> Quelque disproportion qu'il y ait entre deux maisons qui ont les beautés qui leur conviennent, elles ne s'effacent point l'une par l'autre: ce qui fait que Chantilly n'efface point Liancourt, bien qu'il ait infiniment plus de diverses beautés, et que Liancourt n'efface pas aussi Chantilly, c'est que Chantilly a les beautés qui conviennent à la grandeur de Monsieur le Prince, et que Liancourt a les beautés qui conviennent à un particulier, et qu'ils ont chacun de vraies beautés. (*I*, p. 112; cf. maxim 626)

In order to master the art of conversation, one has to apply in a different field this same notion of *convenance* or appropriateness, which now produces an instinctive rightness in the choice of subject-matter, as earlier in the choice of a dwelling:

> Toute sorte de conversation, quelque honnête et quelque spirituelle qu'elle soit, n'est pas également propre à toute sorte d'honnêtes gens: il faut choisir ce qui convient à chacun, et choisir même le temps de le dire; mais s'il y a beaucoup d'art à savoir parler à propos, il n'y en a pas moins à savoir se taire. (*I*, p. 117)

How many people fail to take full advantage of social or professional promotion, because they are unable to bridge the gap between their own unchanged person, and their new dignity!

> Ce changement de notre fortune change souvent notre air et nos manières, et y ajoute l'air de la dignité, qui est toujours faux quand il est trop marqué, et qu'il n'est pas joint et confondu avec l'air que la nature nous a donné: il faut les unir et les mêler ensemble et qu'ils ne paraissent jamais séparés. [...] Combien de lieutenants généraux apprennent à paraître maréchaux de France! Combien de gens de robe répètent inutilement l'air de chancelier, et combien de bourgeoises se donnent l'air de duchesses! (*I*, p. 116)

This idea reappears in various forms throughout the *Réflexions,* culminating in no. 13, 'Du faux', which is largely devoted to the errors of judgement which involve a faulty sense of appropriateness, and mar our conduct on important social occasions:

> Si les hommes ne voulaient exceller que par leurs propres talents, et en
> suivant leurs devoirs, il n'y aurait rien de faux dans leur goût et dans
> leur conduite; ils se montreraient tels qu'ils sont; ils jugeraient des
> choses par leurs lumières, et s'y attacheraient par leur raison; il y aurait
> de la proportion dans leurs vues et dans leurs sentiments; leur goût serait
> vrai, il viendrait d'eux et non pas des autres, et ils le suivraient par
> choix, et non pas par coutume ou par hasard. (*1*, p. 129)

However subtle the criteria involved in such judgements, La
Rochefoucauld suggests that they are all amenable to rational
analysis. Curiously, he has very little to say that is explicit, in this
Réflexion, about the possible influence of vanity, or of other
manifestations of *amour-propre,* in distorting our vision, though it is
constantly present by implication.

It is now clear that in denouncing all kinds of falsity to which
human nature is prone, our author is pursuing not just a negative
goal, a 'demolition', but—indirectly at least—an ideal of truth, of
personal authenticity. His most earnest attempt to define this ideal in
the field of inter-personal relations is found in the fifth of the
Réflexions diverses, 'De la confiance'. Here the discussion centres on
the obligations we may incur when friends and acquaintances entrust
secrets to us. Such *confidences* may subsequently involve us in acute
moral dilemmas; but La Rochefoucauld is unyielding over the
necessity of keeping one's promise of discretion, even at the risk of
losing other friends in the process:

> Cet état est sans doute la plus rude épreuve de la fidélité; mais il ne doit
> pas ébranler un honnête homme: c'est alors qu'il lui est permis de se
> préférer aux autres; son premier devoir est indispensablement de
> conserver le dépôt en son entier, sans en peser les suites; il doit non
> seulement ménager ses paroles et ses tons, il doit encore ménager ses
> conjectures, et ne laisser jamais rien voir, dans ses discours ni dans son
> air, qui puisse tourner l'esprit des autres vers ce qu'il ne veut pas dire.
> (*1*, p. 121)

Yet in the same essay we find a definition of sincerity which is as
equivocal as ever: 'la sincérité est une ouverture du cœur, qui nous
montre tels que nous sommes; c'est un amour de la vérité, une
répugnance à se déguiser, un désir de se dédommager de ses défauts,
et de les diminuer même par le mérite de les avouer' (p. 120).
Human motivation remains ambiguous, if less obviously so, in the
Réflexions as in the *Maximes.* It follows that genuine sincerity must
include sincerity toward oneself, which cannot be achieved without
the insight that leads to self-knowledge. To acquire this is a difficult,
indeed almost heroic task. We have to overcome the many
difficulties we have already seen described in such maxims as: 'Nous
sommes si accoutumés à nous déguiser aux autres qu'enfin nous nous
déguisons à nous-mêmes' (119); or: 'On est quelquefois aussi

différent de soi-même que des autres' (135; cf. 315). Self-knowledge
is not handed to us; it has to be conquered.

   True *honnêteté* is therefore unattainable without true sincerity,
and that in its turn cannot be achieved without a high degree of
lucidity. It is this quality above all that the author of the *Maximes*
strives to promote in his readers: a refusal to lie to oneself, a sharp
focus of self-criticism, capable of detachment and irony, and above
all of recognising the blandishments of *amour-propre,* and of side-
stepping the many traps it is always setting up in our path. What is
usually lacking in men is not the ability but the will to see clearly
within themselves (494). Some will therefore regard such lucidity as
a malediction rather than as a uniquely precious quality, for it
destroys the more naïve forms of happiness that derive from our
facile self-satisfaction (588). This clear insight into oneself, and the
ability to act upon it, are achievements almost as rare as heroism
according to the old chivalrous ideal. Several passages in the
Réflexions stress the rarity of perfect *honnêteté* and of its related
qualities. For instance, the ultimate secrets of the art of conversation
are highly elusive: 'le secret de s'en bien servir est donné à peu de
personnes; ceux même qui en font des règles s'y méprennent
quelquefois' (p. 118). Even rarer is perfect taste: 'Il est très rare, et
presque impossible, de rencontrer cette sorte de bon goût qui sait
donner le prix à chaque chose', for this too can fall victim to *amour-
propre:* 'Cette juste disposition des qualités qui font bien juger ne se
maintient d'ordinaire que sur ce qui ne nous regarde pas
directement' (p. 125). Rare indeed are the individuals who reveal
nothing 'false' in their judgements: 'Ceux-ci sont très rares, puisque,
à parler généralement, il n'y a presque personne qui n'ait de la
fausseté dans quelque endroit de l'esprit ou du goût' (pp. 128-9). It
would be difficult to be more demanding of humanity than is La
Rochefoucauld in these lines.

   It can therefore be said that although many traditional aristocratic
values have been abandoned in the *Maximes,* the idea of the existence
of an élite remains intact. *Honnêteté* is presented throughout La
Rochefoucauld's writings as a difficult art that only a chosen few can
learn and practise to perfection. It can also be seen as 'the life-line
that sustains the unregenerate self in the monstrous sea of *amour-
propre'* (*57,* pp. 240-41). Like Divine Grace in the most rigorous
Jansenist perspective, it seems to be a gift offered only to a
privileged few. That knowledge however should not prevent men of
good will from striving towards the ideal proposed, if they recognise
it as such. La Rochefoucauld appears to expect nothing less than this
effort of humanity, and it is a sign of his respect for man that he
does.

Chapter Four

The Art of the Maxim

Despite some apparent incoherence, La Rochefoucauld remains an impressive thinker, be it only for his remarkable power to convey the contradictions of human experience. His art is elusive, especially in its subtle alliance of form and content. Does the excellence of a successful maxim depend primarily on the incisiveness of the thought, or on the original use of language, or on an inspired combination of the two? The author himself was convinced that ideas alone did not suffice to create a maxim: '...il est aussi ridicule de vouloir faire des sentences, sans en avoir la graine en soi, que de vouloir qu'un parterre produise des tulipes, quoiqu'on n'y ait point semé d'oignons' (505). The aim of these brief inventions is not so much to state a truth as to open up a new angle of vision on that truth (45, pp. 84-6). Their aristocratic air of spontaneity and negligence is deceptive: behind it lay hours of meditation, calculation and experiment, as we see in the transformations undergone by many texts (see above, pp. 21-2). It is above all in their creative use of language that these maxims have remained supreme in the genre that they virtually created. On many occasions, it would not be extravagant to describe La Rochefoucauld as a poet.

It may be appropriate initially to recall the essential ingredients of a successful maxim. Brevity is no doubt the basic requirement, but it must be a brevity charged with meaning; that is, as much brevity as is compatible with the need to record a relatively complex thought-process. A bipolar structure, incorporating some sort of comparison or antithesis, though not found in every example without exception, is present in the vast majority of them, and we must place it among the essentials, or near-essentials, of the genre. Such a juxtaposition will tend to be of an unexpected kind, and may even incorporate a mild obscurity that stimulates the reader's imagination with its 'oracular' quality. In other words, some element of paradox will always be present in a successful maxim, and its function will be to 'turn a truism into an epigram' (45, p. 91). Finally, this epigrammatic quality, which engraves the words on the memory, will be enhanced by the choice of diction: the verbal rhythms and sonorities will contribute, more than may be realised by any but the most perceptive readers, to the fascination, or the provocation, produced by the master practitioner of the maxim.

However, as a genre, the maxim runs the risk of producing irritation as much as enchantment. Even in the case of La Rochefoucauld, a small number of texts are little more than empty platitudes, for example: 'On n'est jamais si heureux ni si malheureux qu'on s'imagine' (49), or especially no. 519: 'La fin du bien est un mal, et la fin du mal est un bien'. (The author may have judged likewise, for this one was never published by him.) Now and again a variant will reveal the relative unimportance of the connotation beside the neatness of the formula. The paradox of 'La confiance de plaire est souvent un moyen de déplaire infailliblement' (622) is an instructive improvement on the version found in two early manuscripts: 'La confiance de plaire est souvent le moyen de plaire infailliblement' (see *3*, p. 194). Mme de Sévigné, in a letter of 14 July 1680, approves of her daughter's proposed reversal of maxim no. 42, so that 'Nous n'avons pas assez de force pour suivre toute notre raison' might become 'Nous n'avons pas assez de raison pour employer toute notre force'. In other words, La Rochefoucauld could occasionally have confessed, as did Mme de Sablé of one of her own efforts: 'Cette sentence n'est que pour faire une sentence' (see *4*, pp. xlix-1 and 560). The thought, in such cases, is subordinate to word-play, as no doubt in no. 128: 'La trop grande subtilité est une fausse délicatesse, et la véritable délicatesse est une solide subtilité'; or in the clumsy no. 407: 'Il s'en faut bien que ceux qui s'attrapent à nos finesses ne nous paraissent aussi ridicules que nous le paraissons à nous-mêmes, quand les autres nous ont attrapés'. (Cf. nos. 96, 270, 355, 576)

The first systematic attempt to codify the 'rules' of La Rochefoucauld's 'word-games' was made in 1908 by Gustave Lanson in chapter IX of *L'Art de la prose* (*38*, pp. 133-9). He shows for instance how skilfully the author sets up a parallel, or a contrast, between two objects or concepts. This will be particularly effective when the two terms are far removed from each other in meaning, as in: 'Il y a des gens qui ressemblent aux vaudevilles, qu'on ne chante qu'un certain temps' (211)—a *vaudeville* was the seventeenth-century equivalent of a 'hit song'—or when one is of a physical, and the other of a moral nature, for instance: 'La flatterie est une fausse monnaie, qui n'a de cours que par notre vanité' (158). A comparison or (more often) a contrast between synonyms, paronyms or cognate words is another fruitful device, adjectives and verbs being particularly effective here as key-words. Two examples must suffice: 'Le ridicule déshonore plus que le déshonneur' (326), and 'Les femmes qui aiment pardonnent plus aisément les grandes indiscrétions que les petites infidélités' (429). Parallels between antonyms can be equally successful: 'L'esprit nous sert quelquefois à faire hardiment des sottises' (415; cf. 451). Occasionally Lanson discovers three such devices at work simultaneously, as in no. 228: 'L'orgueil ne veut pas devoir, et l'amour-propre ne veut pas payer', in which he identifies: 'expression du moral par le physique, opposition des contraires, distinction des synonymes' (*38*, p. 138). In all these examples, in contrast to the 'hollow' formulae referred to in the last paragraph, there is enough solid meaning to refute the charge of mere verbal manipulation. It must already be evident that in all La Rochefoucauld's most successful inventions, the provocative idea and the skilful combination of words are found in equal measure, and in firm alliance. In addition, almost everywhere, we find an element of paradox. This has been defined, in an important study by Jonathan Culler, as 'an apparent contradiction that is dissipated by the very process of understanding' (*15*, p. 28). The same analysis (pp. 35-8) demonstrates that part of the fascination of the *Maximes* lies in the ambiguities arising from the author's failure, or unwillingness, to define his own moral terminology. Paradox, like the word-play with which it is closely associated, can easily be overdone for effect, resulting once again in a certain appearance of gratuitousness, as in: 'On ne devrait s'étonner que de pouvoir encore s'étonner' (384), or: 'Il n'y a point de gens qui aient plus souvent tort que ceux qui ne peuvent souffrir d'en avoir' (386). Further reflection may lead us to recognise an element of genuine insight in the second of these two maxims, whereas the first continues to irritate because its *raison d'être* lies in the word-game rather than in the moral truth expressed.

Another factor that can provoke occasional miscalculation is the author's pursuit of the maximum possible brevity. There are a few maxims in which excessive concentration has produced some degree of obscurity, such as no. 13: 'Notre amour-propre souffre plus impatiemment la condamnation de nos goûts que de nos opinions' or in no. 379: 'Quand notre mérite baisse, notre goût baisse aussi'. (The concept of *goût* is a subtle one, as our author vividly demonstrates in the tenth *Réflexion:* see *46*, pp. 120-40). It may have been to such texts that Le Père Bouhours was referring when he wrote: 'A force de serrer les choses, on les étrangle, et on les étouffe aussi' (quoted in *7*, p. 114). However, a modicum of obscurity, as we have seen, forms part of the attraction of the maxim, reinforcing its 'oracular' quality. Who would complain at being forced to think by the challenging brevity of 'Il y a des héros en mal comme en bien' (185)? Ellipsis is a frequent stylistic feature of the *Maximes,* and generally speaking La Rochefoucauld handles it with assurance, as in no. 38: 'Nous promettons selon nos espérances, et nous tenons selon nos craintes'; or in no. 11: 'Les passions en engendrent souvent qui leur sont contraires: l'avarice produit quelquefois la prodigalité, et la prodigalité l'avarice; et on est souvent ferme par faiblesse, et audacieux par timidité' (cf. *61*, pp. 132-3). A few maxims are quite admirable in their power to convey a wealth of meaning in a limited number of words, for instance no. 168 (quoted above, p. 46, and analysed in *28*, pp. 61-70), or no. 32: 'La jalousie se nourrit dans les doutes, et elle devient fureur, ou elle finit, sitôt qu'on passe du doute à la certitude'. A study of the various *états du texte* will reveal the author's patient search for the perfect formula (see *3*, pp. 19-20).

Attempts have been made to describe and categorize the different 'construction models' used in the *Maximes* (see notably *4*, pp. xliv-xlviii). A statistical analysis reveals that the total number of these models remains relatively small—perhaps not more than twenty in all—and that even to reach this total, some fairly subtle distinctions have to be imposed. Consequently the present attempt at description will confine itself to some of the most basic and readily distinguishable paradigms. For instance, definitions abound in La Rochefoucauld, as in so many authors of the time, reminding us that the late seventeenth century was the first great era of dictionary-making in France. Among the many definitions in the *Maximes,* few are as straightforward as the opening sentence of no. 62: 'La sincérité est une ouverture du cœur.' (At once, however, the author remarks on the rarity of such an uncomplicated disposition in the corrupt heart of man.) Similar in tone, though much more extended, is the definition of love in no. 68: 'Il est difficile de définir l'amour; ce qu'on en peut dire, c'est que, dans l'âme, c'est une passion de régner; dans les esprits, c'est une sympathie; et, dans le corps, ce n'est qu'une envie cachée et délicate de posséder ce que l'on aime après beaucoup de mystères.' It is in *Réflexion* no. V, rather than in maxim no. 62, that La Rochefoucauld attempts to define sincerity (see *1*, p. 120). The suggested motivation appears less and less disinterested as the text progresses. This is the most usual function of definition in La Rochefoucauld: to suggest that the motives associated with the quality defined are by no means as straightforward as men will claim, or believe, them to be. Sometimes great resources of subtlety are brought to bear to this end, as in no. 175 (quoted above, p. 46). Other multiple definitions could be seen as masterpieces of authorial perfidy, for instance, no. 254: 'L'humilité n'est qu'une feinte soumission, dont on se sert pour soumettre les autres; c'est un artifice de l'orgueil, qui s'abaisse pour s'élever; et bien qu'il se transforme en mille manières, il n'est jamais mieux déguisé et plus capable de tromper que lorsqu'il se cache sous la figure de l'humilité'. Even a harmless-looking definition like that of civility (260) is still powerfully suggestive of *amour-propre:* 'La civilité est un désir d'en recevoir et d'être estimé poli.' As for La Rochefoucauld's definitions of feminine virtues, they follow a predictably treacherous pattern: 'La sévérité des femmes est un ajustement et un fard qu'elles ajoutent à leur beauté' (204); 'L'honnêteté des femmes est souvent l'amour de leur réputation et de leur repos' (205).

The last three maxims quoted are disguised examples of a construction we have already noted, namely the negative *ne ... que*, producing what has been called 'reductive definition' or 'restrictive identity'. Its prominence already in the epigraph—'Nos vertus ne sont le plus souvent que des vices déguisés'—serves to underline its ubiquitous presence: it will recur no less than eighty times. Roland Barthes has written of this construction: 'On serait tenté de faire de cette relation déceptive (puisqu'elle *déçoit* l'apparence au profit d'une réalité toujours moins glorieuse) l'expression logique de ce qu'on a appelé le pessimisme de La Rochefoucauld' (*11*, p. 76). It has also been characterised as depicting 'the disillusioned *honnête homme* sitting back and watching the world—his world—go by, while he sardonically notes down all its follies' (*61*, pp. 131-2). The 'reductive definition', much favoured by Augustinian writers such as Nicole, Esprit and Senault (see *33*, pp. 158-9), is a highly effective means of questioning conventional habits of thought, and of setting up unexpected relationships. This systematic negation of accepted wisdom is vigorously set in motion, immediately after the 'reductive' epigraph, by the scorching generalisation of maxim no. 1: 'Ce que nous prenons pour des vertus n'est souvent qu'un assemblage de diverses actions et de divers intérêts que la fortune ou notre industrie savent arranger...' The author usually makes a bald statement incorporating this construction, and then leaves the reader to work out the implications of his 'reductive definition':

> La constance des sages n'est que l'art de renfermer leur agitation dans le cœur. (20)

> La haine pour les favoris n'est autre chose que l'amour de la faveur. (55)

> L'amour de la justice n'est, en la plupart des hommes, que la crainte de souffrir l'injustice. (78)

Some of these maxims seem to imply fierce scorn for humanity, but others are more neutral in tone, for instance: 'La réconciliation avec nos ennemis n'est qu'un désir de rendre notre condition meilleure, une lassitude de la guerre, et une crainte de quelque mauvais événement' (82). Clearly, by supplying three possible explanations instead of just one, La Rochefoucauld has lessened the negative impact of his judgement.

Other types of negative construction are almost as abundant in the *Maximes* as the *ne ... que* form. Nearly every kind of negative in fact is represented, as in the following examples:

> Si nous n'avions point d'orgueil, nous ne nous plaindrions pas de celui des autres. (34)

Il n'y a guère de gens qui ne soient honteux de s'être aimés, quand ils ne s'aiment plus. (71)

On n'aime point à louer, et on ne loue jamais personne sans intérêt. (144)

Il n'est rien de plus naturel ni de plus trompeur que de croire qu'on est aimé. (557)

As we can see here, the powerful negative element in La Rochefoucauld's thought is closely mirrored in his linguistic structures.

Another device which somewhat resembles the 'reductive definition' is what has been called the *distinguo* (*36*, pp. 91-4). Its standard form is that of *oui, mais...* (e.g. 27, 74, 186, 197, 301, 317, 318, 353, etc.), but an occasional variant is *oui, et...* (e.g. 38, 89, 98, 294). The basic function of this construction is to shed new light on men's behaviour through greater subtlety of analysis, by proceding from what is widely known to what is less commonly perceived. Two of the most striking examples of *distinguo* are: 'Nous pardonnons souvent à ceux qui nous ennuient, mais nous ne pouvons pardonner à ceux que nous ennuyons' (304); 'On est quelquefois un sot avec de l'esprit, mais on ne l'est jamais avec du jugement' (456; cf. 361, 490). This mode of investigation is occasionally applied to well-known defects of character or behaviour (e.g. 318, 364, 393), but it more commonly serves to question the true nature of activities and qualities habitually perceived as positive or virtuous, e.g. 'La philosophie triomphe aisément des maux passés et des maux à venir, mais les maux présents triomphent d'elle' (22) or: 'On croit quelquefois haïr la flatterie, mais on ne hait que la manière de flatter' (329). This binary construction is conducive to brevity, but in a few cases a ternary formula achieves a greater subtlety: 'Presque tout le monde prend plaisir à s'acquitter des petites obligations; beaucoup de gens ont de la reconnaissance pour les médiocres; mais il n'y a quasi personne qui n'ait de l'ingratitude pour les grandes' (299). A similar function to that of *distinguo* is performed in quite a number of maxims by constructions introduced by *si*, as in: 'Si l'on juge de l'amour par la plupart de ses effets, il ressemble plus à la haine qu'à l'amitié' (72); 'Si nous résistons à nos passions, c'est plus par leur faiblesse que par notre force' (122; cf. 34, 69, 311, 374, 388).

Some further 'construction models' deserve a brief but honourable mention. Several maxims establish a relationship of proportion between two qualities, which Lanson amused himself by converting into a mathematical equation (*38*, p. 135—a procedure scorned by Lafond, *30*, pp. 133-4). The text he chose for this

experiment was no. 67: 'La bonne grâce est au corps ce que le bon
sens est à l'esprit'. A similarly abstract quality characterises some
other maxims cast in this mould: 'L'élévation est au mérite ce que la
parure est aux belles personnes' (401); 'L'amour est à l'âme de celui
qui aime ce que l'âme est au corps qu'elle anime' (576); 'La sagesse
est à l'ame ce que la santé est pour le corps' (541). Only one use of
this device conveys a more typically pessimistic message. Some
condemned prisoners, writes La Rochefoucauld, put on an air of
bravado and indifference to death, 'de sorte qu'on peut dire que cette
constance et ce mépris sont à leur esprit ce que le bandeau est à leurs
yeux' (21). Other maxims establish a relationship of superiority,
inferiority or equality between qualities or actions, for instance:
'L'amour-propre est plus habile que le plus habile homme du monde'
(4); 'Il n'est pas si dangereux de faire du mal à la plupart des
hommes que de leur faire trop de bien' (238); 'Il est aussi ordinaire
de voir changer les goûts, qu'il est extraordinaire de voir changer les
inclinations (252; cf. 115)—one of a number of texts that might
benefit from a clarification of terminology. We are not far removed
here from the extended simile, the function of which in the *Maximes*
will be examined shortly. Finally, we have already considered the
'compensation structure' (see above, pp. 48-9), which provides a
powerful counterweight to the prevailing pessimism, together with
some admirable stylistic successes. Here are two further illustrations
of the author's dexterity with this particular formula: 'Quelque
découverte que l'on ait faite dans le pays de l'amour-propre, il y
reste encore bien des terres inconnues' (3); 'Quelque disposition
qu'ait le monde à mal juger, il fait encore plus souvent grâce au faux
mérite qu'il ne fait injustice au véritable' (455). This structure is
favoured by La Rochefoucauld both as a thinker and as a style-
conscious artist.

   Most of the texts quoted in this chapter provide examples of the
rhetorical figure most constantly employed by our author, namely
antithesis. In fact, we find it in some form in the majority of his
maxims, for it is fundamental both to this literary genre and to the
whole rhetoric of French classicism. Barthes has called it 'une force
universelle de signification' (*11*, p. 78; cf. *42*, pp. 161-2). Like his
contemporaries, La Rochefoucauld uses an abundance of antitheses in
argument; they are sometimes carefully patterned, as in this passage
from *Réflexion* no. XVIII: 'Quelles personnes auraient commencé de
s'aimer, si elles s'étaient vues d'abord comme on se voit dans la suite
des années? Mais quelles personnes aussi se pourraient séparer, si
elles se revoyaient comme on s'est vu la première fois?' (*1*, p. 150).
In the *Maximes,* the antithetical structure presents a constant
challenge, forcing the reader to revalue the first half of the statement
—which may have seemed unexceptionable, or even banal—in the

light of a newly-added truth, as for instance in: 'Chacun dit du bien
de son cœur, / et personne n'en ose dire de son esprit' (98), or in:
'Tout le monde se plaint de sa mémoire, / et personne ne se plaint de
son jugement' (89—see *9*, pp. 233-6). Thanks to the use of antithesis,
reality is shown to be quite different from commonly-accepted
belief: 'Il faut de plus grandes vertus pour soutenir la bonne fortune
que la mauvaise' (25); 'La vérité ne fait pas tant de bien dans le
monde que ses apparences y font de mal' (64). Our author's pursuit
of 'bilateral symmetry' produces a constant supply of finely balanced
antitheses, single or double: 'L'intérêt, qui aveugle les uns, fait la
lumière des autres' (40); and: 'Il y a des reproches qui louent, et des
louanges qui médisent' (148). The mirror effect (ABBA) produced in
this last text forms a rhetorical figure known as chiasmus, quite a
few examples of which can be located (e.g. nos. 128, 251, 355, 400,
497, 561). Becoming more ambitious, La Rochefoucauld produces
effects of symmetry which could be described as 'trilateral' or even
'multi-lateral' (see *61*, pp. 55 ff.): 'Il n'y a point d'accidents si
malheureux dont les habiles gens ne tirent quelque avantage, ni de si
heureux que les imprudents ne puissent tourner à leur préjudice' (59,
cf. 16). Such texts may be considered as virtuoso showpieces; but
generally speaking, La Rochefoucauld is careful not to allow his
prolific antitheses to become too repetitive or too mechanical. Quite
a simple modification of a construction may produce an impression
of variety, as in no. 437: 'On ne doit pas juger du mérite d'un
homme par ses grandes qualités, mais par l'usage qu'il en sait faire',
the prepositional phrase being replaced in the second instance by a
clause, rather than exactly matched; or as in no. 111: 'Plus on aime
une maîtresse, et plus on est prêt de la haïr', where the simple
transitive verb gives way to an adjective introducing an infinitive.
(see *61*, pp. 60-61) Lanson's neat mathematical equations do scant
justice to La Rochefoucauld's ability to surprise us. As Jean Lafond
has pointed out (*30*, pp. 133-5), Lanson's description of no. 294 as
'une partie carrés de verbes' suggests a flawless regularity which, if
achieved, would have produced a mere platitude. Perfect symmetry
would require that this maxim: 'Nous aimons toujours ceux qui nous
admirent, et nous n'aimons pas toujours ceux que nous admirons',
should end differently, with 'ceux qui ne nous admirent pas'. It is
such small variants as these that distinguish a La Rochefoucauld from
an abbé d'Ailly. In no. 248: 'La magnanimité méprise tout, pour
avoir tout', the word *tout* figures in both parts of the antithesis, but it
does not refer to the same totality the second time, for it suggests
renown rather than power or wealth. Odette de Mourgues has
pointed out that antithesis, since it corresponds so closely to our
mental habits, is only too readily accepted by the listener or reader,
and that to be fully effective, it requires to be 'presented in a special

way' (*47,* pp. 78-9). This is the case in no. 289: 'La simplicité
affectée est une imposture délicate', where the noun and the adjective
jar together in each case, resulting in a near-oxymoron, but
particularly in the second pair, which produces 'a strange alliance of
strong disapproval and gentle praise'. Such unexpected combinations
of words not only give aesthetic pleasure, but prevent us from
exercising too simplistic a moral judgement.

Mental 'shocks' administered in this way indicate that for La
Rochefoucauld, antithesis is inseparable from paradox; this often
consists, so far as the reader is concerned, in finding an unforeseen
link between the two opposing poles of the antithesis. *Amour-propre,*
with its endless contradictions (563), is a source of perpetual
paradox. The human heart is an inexhaustible fount of warring
passions, each of which tends to engender its opposite (10, 11, 478,
492). Antithesis and parallelism are used in many maxims to
underscore the paradoxical aspects of men's behaviour, for instance
in: 'Les hommes ne sont pas seulement sujets à perdre le souvenir des
bienfaits et des injures: ils haïssent même ceux qui les ont obligés, et
cessent de haïr ceux qui leur ont fait des outrages' (14; cf. 155, 596).
A common source of paradox is in the reversal of a truism. One of
our author's standard procedures is to turn a widely accepted
judgement on its head, in order to produce 'an almost simultaneous
destruction and reconstruction of received opinion' (*48,* p. 45). This
form of paradox is a useful pointer to the complexity of moral truth:
there is a *contre-vérité* to be set beside so many proverbs and
truisms, and La Rochefoucauld is wonderfully adept at finding and
expressing it. Once again, however, the effectiveness of the 'mild
shock' will depend as much on the choice of words as on the
piquancy of the 'reversed idea', as can be seen in: 'Qui vit sans folie
n'est pas si sage qu'il croit' (209); 'La plupart des amis dégoûtent de
l'amitié, et la plupart des dévots dégoûtent de la dévotion' (427; cf.
25, 29, 90, 136, 175, 238, etc.) 'Paradoxical reversal' is another
procedure in which language and thought conclude an unexpected but
fruitful alliance. Given the unpredictable perversity of men's
conduct, it is not surprising to find that the same psychological cause
produces the opposite effect to that anticipated, or that apparently
opposed causes can produce similar effects. Nevertheless, a well-
chosen form of words will greatly enhance the effect of surprise, as
in: 'Rien n'empêche tant d'être naturel que l'envie de le paraître'
(431); or 'N'aimer guère en amour est un moyen assuré pour être
aimé' (636; cf. 426, 475). Another paradoxical theme which emerges
here and there in the *Maximes* is that of *le trompeur trompé.* There
is the theme: 'L'intention de ne jamais tromper nous expose à être
souvent trompés' (118; cf. 117, 119), and the counter-theme: 'Le vrai
moyen d'être trompé, c'est de se croire plus fin que les autres' (127;

cf. 125, 126, 129). The desire to sharpen to the maximum the effects of paradox explains these *tours de force* of brevity that La Rochefoucauld often achieves (see especially nos. 102, 111, 253, 289, 444, 445.)

Paradox is what asserts itself at the end of various maxims renowned for their 'sting in the tail', that is, for the unexpected final word or phrase that obliges us to reassess all that has gone before: 'Nous avons tous assez de force pour supporter les maux / d'autrui' (19); 'Ce qui fait que les amants et les maîtresses ne s'ennuyent point d'être ensemble, c'est qu'ils parlent toujours / d'eux-mêmes' (312); 'Ce qui nous empêche souvent de nous abandonner à un seul vice est que nous en avons / plusieurs' (195; cf. 93, 96, 110, 196, 275, 397, 428, 451, 583). These terminal *pointes* provide fine illustrations of our author's sardonic wit and humour. We have already seen this talent at work at the expense of the other sex (see above, pp. 61-2). Though many of these quips may be judged tasteless today, some of them reveal a genuine satirical talent, and it is often the form of words rather than the substance that is entertaining: 'Une honnête femme est comme un trésor caché; celui qui l'a trouvé fait fort bien de ne pas s'en vanter' (552; cf. 131, 368, 396); La Rochefoucauld's keen perception of the affinity of opposites, in other words his sense of paradox, is essential to his talent as a humorist, as well as to his acuity as a moralist. One could quote plenty of other texts from the *Maximes* that offer humorous entertainment; most of them are connected with 'the battle of the sexes' (see also 73, 76, 340, 369, 408, 429, 466).

We are so used to thinking of La Rochefoucauld as an abstract, analytical, 'classical' *moraliste* that a cursory reading of the *Maximes* may not reveal the importance of the imagery—simile, metaphor and personification—that this work contains. The similes, it is true, are more often remarkable for their aptness than for their originality; they focus most often on man's place in the natural world and his subjection to its laws and processes (*47*, pp. 83-4). Only a few are disappointingly commonplace. Wealth, we are told in no. 520, tends to nourish and propagate crime, 'comme le bois entretient le feu' (cf. 380). A rather larger number of comparisons, on the other hand, are of a quite unexpected order, and as a result they may appear humorously incongruous, for example no. 382, according to which 'Nos actions sont comme les bouts-rimés, que chacun rapporte à ce qui lui plaît' (cf. nos. 76, 211, 292, 368). However, few of La Rochefoucauld's similes strike one as completely gratuitous, or as mere embellishments: nearly all of them are lucid and instructive, lending power and precision to the thought, sometimes virtually constituting that thought. This could be said of two of the most often quoted similes (171, 182). An image may serve to confer some originality on a truism, such as this remark: 'Les rois font des hommes comme des pièces de monnaie; ils les font valoir ce qu'ils veulent, et l'on est forcé de les recevoir selon leur cours, et non pas selon leur véritable prix' (603). What could be more vividly explanatory than the simile used to illustrate the extrordinary combination of lucidity and blindness that characterises *amour-propre:* 'Cette obscurité épaisse qui le cache à lui-même, n'empêche pas qu'il ne voie parfaitement ce qui est hors de lui: en quoi il est semblable à nos yeux, qui découvrent tout et sont aveugles seulement pour eux-mêmes' (563)?

Most of La Rochefoucauld's comparisons would qualify as 'figures justes' in that they derive from, and bring together, realms of experience already familiar to his readers. The natural world provides an obvious source of such imagery. We have already encountered rivers flowing into the sea, which itself provides two extended similes. The first is with *amour,* a parallel to which *Réflexion* VI is devoted: here the author is at pains to show how perfectly the simile fits: 'l'un et l'autre ont une inconstance et une infidélité égales' (*1,* p. 122). The other comparison is with *amour-propre,* forming a poetic epilogue to no. 563: 'La mer en est une image sensible, et l'amour-propre trouve dans le flux et le reflux de ses vagues continuelles une fidèle expression de la succession turbulente de ses penseés et de ses éternels mouvements'. In both cases, the simile vividly conveys the impression of restless movement, of ebb and flow, which La Rochefoucauld attributes to both these psychological forces. Other sources of comparisons in the realm of nature include the spring blossom on fruit trees (274), trees in general (594)—a parallel which our author elaborates at some length in no. 505—and plants, which come in for similar treatment in no. 344: 'La plupart des hommes ont, comme les plantes, des propriétés cachées que le hasard fait découvrir.' When Nature's delicate processes break down, the result is physical illness and its accompanying fevers. This comparison appears in several maxims, and notably in one which stresses its absolute appropriateness: 'La plus juste comparaison qu'on puisse faire de l'amour, c'est celle de la fièvre: nous n'avons non plus de pouvoir sur l'un que sur l'autre, soit pour sa violence, ou pour sa durée' (638; cf. 188, 193, 271, 300, 392). Some other related similes are derived from medicine; we have already referred more than once to no. 182, with which could be associated nos. 194, 288 and 344. Trade and commerce provide a significant number of comparisons, enabling our *grand seigneur* to castigate mankind for lacking that vital attribute of the nobleman, disinterestedness. The 'seminal' maxim for this theme has already been quoted (83; see above, p. 25). Here the term *commerce* is fruitfully ambiguous, preserving both its seventeenth-century sense of 'social relationship' (as in nos. 77 and 90), and its more modern meaning, which is confirmed by the verb *gagner* at the end. Trading also supplies the image for no. 158, and above all for no. 223, where once again it forms the very core of the argument (see above, p. 25; cf. nos. 225, 236). A more traditional image is evoked in no. 191, that of *homo viator*, of life as a journey; but how far removed it is in its message from the sturdy Christian optimism with which it is usually associated: 'On peut dire que les vices nous attendent, dans le cours de la vie, comme des hôtes chez qui il faut successivement loger; et je doute que l'expérience nous les fît éviter, s'il nous était permis de faire deux fois le même chemin.' Finally, the most perfectly chosen and executed simile in the *Maximes,* in the judgement of several critics (see *28,* pp. 110-13; *44,* pp. 128-9), is found in no. 276: 'L'absence diminue les médiocres passions, et augmente les grandes, comme le vent éteint les bougies, et allume le feu.' Here it is the absolute appropriateness of the image, in all its details, that renews the traditional comparison of love with fire, already hackneyed in La Rochefoucauld's day. (A more modest aesthetic success of the same order is achieved in no. 75).

It is difficult to draw a sharp dividing line, when studying the *Maximes,* between simile, metaphor and personification. Some quite explicit comparisons dispense with the introductory *comme* (e.g. 158, 204, 293, 368); and some examples of a construction we studied earlier, involving a relationship of proportion (e.g. 21, 218, 274, 401), could be regarded as disguised similes, as indeed could the celebrated no. 26: 'Le soleil ni la mort ne se peuvent regarder fixement'. In most cases, however, the use of metaphor in the *Maximes* is readily identifiable, and aesthetically effective. La Rochefoucauld, like all truly creative writers, could on occasion breathe new life into over-used images. The 'terres inconnues' of no. 3 would be a felicitous invention, even without the allusion to Mlle de Scudéry's *Carte du Tendre.* Certain metaphors are placed strategically, for instance at the very end of a maxim: 'Quelque soin que l'on prenne de couvrir ses passions par des apparences de piété et d'honneur, elles paraissent toujours au travers de ces voiles' (12). Our author does not always shun the most hackneyed metaphorical themes, such as the lucky star (58, 165) or the sparkling gem (354), but he often succeeds in putting his own personal stamp on them. Sometimes images are suggested without being made explicit, as in no. 222: 'Il n'y a guère de personnes qui, dans le premier penchant de l'âge, ne fassent connaître par où leur corps et leur esprit doivent défaillir.' The combination of 'penchant' (in its now archaic sense of 'declivity') and of 'défaillir' evokes a veiled image of collapse. The same kind of metaphorical suggestion is at work several times in no. 230: 'Rien n'est si contagieux que l'exemple, et nous ne faisons jamais de grands biens ni de grands maux qui n'en produisent de semblables. Nous imitons les bonnes actions par émulation, et les mauvaises par la malignité de notre nature, que la honte retenait prisonnier, et que l'exemple met en liberté.' Here we are on the borderline between original imagery—personification as much as metaphor—and the conventional metaphoric usage of everyday speech. As for the more explicit and extended type of metaphor, apart from the 'turbulent sea' images referred to above as simile, there is the comparison with the ocean (extended but less explicit) in no. 297, quoted above (p. 36); and two other notable marine metaphors, that of the legendary fish, 'la rémore qui a la force d'arrêter les plus grands vaisseaux', and that of the becalmed ocean, *la bonace,* so much more feared in the days of sail (see 630, quoted above, p. 35; and also *Réflexion* VI, in *1,* p. 112). A somewhat comparable text (510—also quoted above, p. 28) is an extended dramatisation of the initial metaphor, 'l'intérêt est l'âme de l'amour-propre', which brilliantly exploits the etymological connection between *âme* and *animation.* In general, there is a richer repository of metaphor to be found in the *Réflexions* than in the *Maximes.* Foremost among them from this point of view is no. 11, 'Du rapport des hommes avec les animaux', an extended metaphorical bestiary of remarkable ingenuity, not to say extravagance. In the next piece, 'De l'origine des maladies', a rather similar feat of the imagination is apparently intended to be taken literally: it produces a catalogue of alleged psychosomatic illnesses that leaves the twentieth-century reader somewhat bemused. La Rochefoucauld is nothing if not a resourceful and varied author.

However noteworthy may be the function of simile and metaphor, that of personification is surely even more apparent. In the rather unlikely genre of the maxim, La Rochefoucauld demonstrated the same sense of the theatrical that characterised many great contemporary authors. It has been rightly observed that 'les personnifications occupent une place privilégiée dans les *Maximes*' (*4,* p. liii). Their frequent occurrence helps to ensure a certain dynamism and dramatic cohesion in a work characterised in the first place by fragmentation and analytical abstraction (see above all *59*). Some of the pre-1678 revisions had the effect of sharpening a personification (see e.g. *3,* pp. 11-12, 19-20, 75), though occasionally such inventions are seen to diminish and even disappear during the same process (*3,* pp. 32-3, 102-103). Sometimes La Rochefoucauld introduces his personifications in a clear and direct statement, sometimes by more stealthy means. There is only a hint of this figure in texts such as no. 43: 'L'homme croit souvent se conduire lorsqu'il est conduit, et pendant que par son esprit il tend à un but, son coeur l'entraîne insensiblement à un autre'; or in no. 297, where the personification is almost as muted as the sea metaphor referred to above. The first thirteen maxims contain an exceptional concentration of such figures, in texts of varying degrees of elaboration and explicitness, concerning both *amour-propre* and the passions in general. The key instrument of personification is of course the verb, and our degree of awareness of this figure may depend on how we 'read' the verb, that is, in a more or less literal or alternatively more abstract sense. May an expression such as 'l'avarice *produit* quelquefois la prodigalité' (11), or 'l'espérance *sert* à nous mener...' (168), be called a personification or not? (Cf. the verbs: *ont* in nos. 9 and 255, *suit* in no. 207, *représentent* in no. 282). However, the verb's function is more clear-cut in such examples as no. 200: 'La vertu n'irait pas loin si la vanité ne lui tenait compagnie' or no. 33: 'L'orgueil se dédommage et ne perd rien, lors même qu'il renonce à la vanité.' (Cf. nos. 32, 109, 169, 275 and 494, among many others.) Less commonly, the word embodying the personification may be an adjective, as in no. 4: 'L'amour-propre est plus habile que le plus habile homme du monde'; or a noun, as in no. 102: 'L'esprit est toujours la dupe du cœur.' Many of these figurative expressions achieve a marked degree of animation. Pride and *amour-propre* have an assertive will of their own, and haggle like hard-nosed merchants: 'L'orgueil ne veut pas devoir, et l'amour-propre ne veut pas payer' (228; cf. 225). False humility has become a master of disguise (254), and our vices masquerade both as hosts and as guests (191, 192). One particularly striking personification comes close to allegory: 'La vieillesse est un tyran qui défend, sur peine de la vie, tous les plaisirs de la jeunesse' (461). Some of the most elaborate personifications have been described—not always convincingly—as forms of 'nuclear allegory' (*61*, pp. 107-109). La Rochefoucauld's most ambitious essay in personification is undoubtedly the 'grand portrait' of *amour-propre* (no. 563, already analysed at length above, pp. 34-6), in which he traces its manifold convolutions and metamorphoses. It has been well said that 'le lecteur de La Rochefoucauld prend l'habitude d'un univers animé, vivant, où toutes ces entités que sont l'amour-propre, l'intérêt, l'humeur, la fortune, l'amour, les vertus, les vices ou les passions apparaissent comme autant de personnes agissantes et douées d'une volonté propre' (*4*, p. liii). Such a form of dramatisation often serves to mitigate the various paradoxes on which the *Maximes* are founded.

Finally, metaphor and personification are brought together in the theme of 'all the world's a stage', which can be discovered (or at least detected) from time to time in this work. Most often its presence is veiled or latent, as in: 'Tous les sentiments ont chacun un ton de voix, des gestes et des mines qui leur sont propres, et ce rapport, bon ou mauvais, agréable ou désagréable, est ce qui fait que les personnes plaisent ou déplaisent' (255; cf. 119, 256, 282). This notion of role-playing becomes more explicit in two briefer texts; 'L'intérêt parle toutes sortes de langues, et joue toutes sortes de personnages, même celui de désintéressé' (39) and: 'L'esprit ne saurait jouer longtemps le personnage du cœur' (108)—two maxims in which the reader is left to puzzle out the precise meaning. Only once does the *theatrum mundi* theme blaze forth triumphantly, and even then in a text that did not survive beyond 1665: 'L'orgueil, comme lassé de ses artifices et de ses différentes métamorphoses, après avoir joue tout seul tous les personnages de la comédie humaine, se montre avec un visage naturel, et se découvre par la fierté: de sorte qu'à proprement parler, la fierté est l'éclat et la déclaration de l'orgueil' (568). Faced with this spectacle of universal play-acting, the *honnête homme* has a clear duty: to try to counteract the masquerading through his own genuineness and truthfulness. Affectation, for La Rochefoucauld, was one of the commonest human defects, and one of the most difficult to cure: 'Rien n'empêche tant d'être naturel que l'envie de le paraître' (431).

The prominence of imagery in many maxims is undeniable, but it must not obscure the primary source of their excellence, which is La Rochefoucauld's rare gift for 'arranging words' in combinations that are satisfying both intellectually and aesthetically. Some form of verbal patterning, even if minimal, is no doubt essential to any text that we may call a maxim; form and content are interdependent, though there seem to be no fixed rules to govern either. One may suspect that in some cases it was the form of words that virtually created the idea in the author's mind (see, e.g., nos. 151, 155, 177, 201, 322, 400, 462). We have already studied some forms of verbal patterning, for instance those connected with antithesis; and a very few examples of repetition and its varied effects must suffice now to remind ourselves of its paramount importance. The most straightforward (binary) forms of patterning almost always embody an antithesis. To quote a typical example: 'La modération est la langueur et la paresse de l'âme, comme l'ambition en est l'activité et l'ardeur' (293). It is in some of the longer texts that more cumulative forms of repetition may be found: 'On pleure pour avoir la réputation d'être tendre; on pleure pour être plaint; on pleure pour être pleuré; enfin, on pleure pour éviter la honte de ne pleurer pas' (233). In his shorter maxims, La Rochefoucauld is particularly partial to the A + B / A + B type of construction, as in no. 294: 'Nous aimons toujours ceux qui nous admirent, et nous n'aimons pas toujours ceux que nous admirons.' Here as elsewhere (e.g. no. 304), it is the minor variant—in this case, the *qui / que* opposition—that averts the risk of monotony, as does the reversal of subject and object in no. 561: 'Un homme à qui personne ne plaît est bien plus malheureux que celui qui ne plaît à personne'. In this last example, the 'meaning' is again almost inseparable from the form of words; sound and sense are in close alliance (cf. 22, 38, 67, etc.) Sometimes the 'variant' will take on the form of chiasmus, as in no. 497: 'Il ne sert de rien d'être jeune sans être belle, ni d'être belle sans être jeune' (cf. 400, 490. For many other examples of verbal patterning, see *61,* pp. 55-113, *passim*)

The question of alliteration, of which some critics claim to find many cases in the *Maximes* (e.g. *45,* pp. 87-8), is a more tricky one. To some extent, the alliteration results inevitably from the repetition of the same words, or one of its paronyms. In other cases, it may be accidental, as probably in no. 607, with its prominent 'p' and 'v' sounds (quoted above, p. 23), or in 'L'honnêteté des femmes est souvent l'amour de leur *r*éputation et de leur *r*epos (205; cf. the triple *-eur* sound in no. 61). One is more inclined to see the alliteration as calculated in the closing lines, just quoted, of no. 233; but here, too, repetition is the prime factor. There is no need to investigate further examples of word-patterning: this form of symmetry is basic to the art of La Rochefoucauld, and the most important ingredient, from the aesthetic point of view, of the *Maximes.*

However, we shall not find perfect unity of style, any more than perfect unity of thought, in La Rochefoucauld. His writings display diverse tendencies: in particular, they stand astride the two main stylistic categories usually applied to seventeenth-century French literature, namely 'baroque' and 'classical'. The 'baroque' elements could be seen as a temptation yielded to by the immature writer, which he later outgrew; but La Rochefoucauld's work would be much the poorer without them. Those critics who define 'baroque' in terms of theme and subject-matter, as well as style, point to certain motifs that are quite prominent in our author. All of them are grouped around two key concepts, which are: inconstancy—the essential instability of human nature and experience; and ostentation—man's unceasing attempts to impose a view of himself in a world of deceptive appearances. From this point of view, a convincing example would be maxim no. 175 ('La constance en amour est une inconstance perpétuelle...') which, although we were tempted to dismiss it earlier as a 'witty quibble' (p. 46), does in fact develop its paradox with an ingenious persistence typical of the 'baroque' aesthetic, based on surprise rather than on the 'classical' concept of harmony. However, in order to study this aspect of La Rochefoucauld in its most visible form, we must turn to the *Réflexions diverses,* and to certain of the longer texts among the

Maximes, in particular to the extended 'portrait' of *amour-propre* in no. 563.

The most striking feature of this already familiar passage, when we compare it to nearly all the maxims that surround it, is its extraordinary linguistic profusion and dynamism. It comprises a seemingly inexhaustible succession of personifications and similes, depicting *amour-propre* (here identified with the totality of man's consciousness) in its struggle to survive. Given its essentially predatory nature, it can do this only by overcoming and devouring everything it encounters on its path. This demonic creature appears related to both the mythical divinities which, according to Jean Rousset's classic analysis in *La Littérature de l'âge baroque en France* (1953), form the most potent symbols of the 'baroque', namely Proteus and Circé, with their supernatural powers of (self-) metamorphosis. La Rochefoucauld's 'monster' exists in a perpetual state of frenetic activity and flux, for with all its inner contradictions it cannot endure any form of repose. Accordingly, throughout this text, the most dynamic linguistic element is provided by the verbs, of which we find some notable sequences and repetitions: 'Dans ses plus grands intérêts et dans ses plus importantes affaires, où la violence de ses souhaits appelle toute son attention, il voit, il sent, il entend, il imagine, il soupçonne, il devine tout...[...] Il est dans tous les états de la vie et dans toutes les conditions, il vit partout et il vit de tout, il vit de rien...' Here it is the language, rather than the intellectual content which wears a little thin after a time, that forms the essential *raison d'être* of the passage. Indeed, La Rochefoucauld seems to become intoxicated with words, and we find him indulging in a veritable 'fantaisie verbale' (*4,* p. 1v). At the same time, his description of life as constant metamorphosis reinforces, from the thematic point of view, the 'baroque' character of this text. Other passages of the *Maximes* and the *Réflexions diverses,* in their somewhat extravagant use of language—of imagery, in particular—offer less spectacular but still notable examples of the 'baroque' aesthetic. Most striking among them are maxims 510 and 630, and *réflexions* nos. VI, IX, XI and XII.

However, all these texts remained unpublished during the author's lifetime, or were withdrawn from publication. The 'grand portrait' (563) appears to have attracted little attention, either in Sercy's anthology of 1659-1660 or at the head of the 1665 edition of the *Maximes.* Other texts were truncated and rewritten, so as to eliminate virtually all the features that we would describe as 'baroque'. The most striking illustration of this process is found in the case of no. 254, which began in the earliest manuscripts, and largely survived into the 1665 edition, as an extended 'portrait' of pride masquerading as humility. Here it achieves 'transformations' comparable, on a much more modest scale, to those of *amour-propre* in no. 563, the name of Proteus being explicitly introduced this time into the text. However, from 1666 onwards, this 'maxim' is reduced to some fifty words of descriptive definition, in which the personification survives, but only just, in a simplified and more abstract form (see *3*, pp. 102-103). These revisions indicate that it was the evolving concept of the maxim, towards a lucid, somewhat abstract but always provocative brevity, that directed the author towards a form of writing of the kind that we call 'classical'. In addition to the brevity, the relevant qualities include the analytical clarity essential to the 'unmasking' process (this despite a certain opacity in the use of psychological language), plus impersonality (the progressive banishment of *le moi*) and the 'pre-established harmony' embodied in the concept of 'figures justes', or well-proportioned images. These were the stylistic qualities most appreciated by the public that La Rochefoucauld addressed in the salons of his day. In the three or four hundred most successful creations among the *Maximes*, he developed them to perfection. As Jean Lafond has written (*30*, p. 195):

> Le classicisme de l'œuvre est épuration dans la mesure où il est stylisation, le style étant la distance à laquelle on se tient de soi-même ou de son œuvre, la marque privilégiée de la maîtrise que l'on exerce sur son objet. Les *Maximes* nous renvoient l'image d'un écrivain dont l'ambition fut d'imposer un style à sa pensée, comme à sa forme.

Conclusion

The difficulties we have encountered in the course of this brief study point to one fact above all: the works of La Rochefoucauld, with the *Maximes* as their centre, form a disconcertingly complex body of writing, subject to changing and often contradictory interpretations. There is no consensus among scholars about this author's basic intentions. In particular, the dichotomy between Augustinian rigour and worldly compromise is hard to resolve. Our only comfort is to discover that La Rochefoucauld was not the only individual of his time and *milieu* to combine Jansenist moral pessimism with an indulgent interest in aesthetics, in worldly distractions, and in how to achieve the pleasurable co-existence of warring individualities. In spite of the trenchant tone of many of his maxims, his hostility to any rigorous *esprit de système* is clear and undeniable. 'Was he ever a thinker?' some critics will ask; or was he not above all an expert manipulator of words? It is difficult to deny altogether the accolade of 'thinker' to a man whose writings have provoked so many vigorous thoughts in numberless readers. Possibly the most helpful contribution of recent criticism to an understanding of these complexities is the notion, suggested particularly by Jean Lafond, of the simultaneous presence in La Rochefoucauld's thought of separate levels, compartments, and *éclairages*. The empiricism of the *Maximes* is bound up with this fragmented form, and it is this quality which enables him to grasp and express the disconcerting paradoxes of human behaviour, and the Protean aspects of personality unveiled by the monstrous evolutions of *amour-propre*. This important element of modernity, together with the remarkable freshness of his language—and an almost complete absence of archaisms—ensures that La Rochefoucauld remains stimulating, and wholly accessible, to twentieth-century readers.

Despite occasional signs of nostalgia for an ideal world of chivalry as opposed to the actual world of *amour-propre,* La Rochefoucauld remains a thoroughgoing realist. The practical result of his Augustinian pessimism is an overriding urge for lucidity, and his essential message for his readers concerns the necessity for vigilance over our own desires and emotions, in order to recognise and if possible frustrate the ruses of *amour-propre*. It may be a sadly persistent truth of experience that 'l'esprit est toujours la dupe du cœur' (102), but this is no immutable fatality. La Rochefoucauld is in no way a didactic writer—he always prefers description and analysis to exhortation—but the desired effect of his aggressive moral probing is to produce in his readers the kind of awareness that will help to thwart the deceptive urges of self-love. The 'demasking' process therefore has a humanitarian goal: it may or not succeed, but aims to enhance our capacity for sincerity and truth towards ourselves.

Bibliography

Books, except where otherwise stated, are published in Paris.

A: Currently available editions

1. *Maximes,* ed. Jean-Pol Caput, Nouveaux Classiques Larousse, 1975.

2. *Œuvres complètes,* édition revue et augmentée, by J. Marchand and L. Martin-Chauffier, Gallimard, Bibliothèque de la Pléiade, 1964.

3. *Réflexions ou sentences et maximes morales. Réflexions diverses.* Présentées avec leurs variantes par Dominique Secrétan, Droz, 1967 (Textes littéraires français, no. 141).

4. *Maximes,* ed. Jacques Truchet, troisième édition revue et augmentée, Classiques Garnier, 1983.

5. *Maximes et Réflexions diverses,* ed. Jean Lafond, deuxième édition revue et augmentée, Gallimard, 1984 ('Folio', no. 728).

6. *Maximes,* ed. Jean Rohou, Librairie Générale Française, 1991 (Livre de poche classique, no. 4486).

7. *Moralistes du XVIIe siècle, de Pibrac à Dufresny.* Édition établie sous la direction de Jean Lafond. Laffont, 1992 (Collection 'Bouquins'). [La Rochefoucauld, *Maximes et Réflexions diverses,* ed. André-Alain Morello, pp. 103-240]

B. Some Recommended Critical Studies

8. Adam, Antoine. *Histoire de la littérature française au XVIIe siècle,* t. IV, Domat, 1954, pp. 81-115.

9. Ansmann, Liane. *Die 'Maximen' von La Rochefoucauld.* Munich, Fink, 1972, 315 pp.

10. Baker, Susan Read. *Collaboration et originalité chez La Rochefoucauld.* Florida University Press, 1980, 135 pp.

11. Barthes, Roland. 'La Rochefoucauld. *Réflexions ou sentences et maximes',* in *Le Degré zéro de l'écriture, suivi de Nouveaux Essais critiques,* Seuil, 1972, pp. 69-88.

12. Bénichou, Paul. 'La Démolition du héros', in *Morales du Grand Siècle,* Gallimard, 1948, pp. 97-111.

13. Bénichou, Paul. 'L'intention des *Maximes*', in *L'Écrivain et ses travaux,* José Corti, 1967, pp. 3-37.

14. Coulet, Henri. 'La Rochefoucauld, ou la peur d'être dupe', in *Hommage au Doyen Étienne Gros,* Gap, 1959, pp. 105-112.

15. Culler, Jonathan. 'Paradox and the Language of Morals in La Rochefoucauld', *The Modern Language Review,* LXVIII, 1 (1973), 28-39.

16. Delft, Louis van. 'La Rochefoucauld moraliste mondain', *Studi Francesi,* XXI (1980), 415-25.

17. Delft, Louis van. *Le Moraliste classique. Essai de définition et de typologie.* Geneva, Droz, 1982, 405 pp.

18. Doubrovsky, Serge. *Parcours critique.* Paris, Éditions Galilée, 1980, 233 pp. ['Vingt propositions sur l'amour-propre. De Lacan à La Rochefoucauld', pp. 203-224].

19. Fine, Peter Martin. *Vauvenargues and La Rochefoucauld.* Manchester University Press, 1974, 163 pp.

20. Ford, Barbara, J. 'The evocative power of the maxim. La Rochefoucauld and Proust', *Romance Notes,* XXV (1984-1985), 169-74.

21. Furber, Donald. 'The Myth of *amour-propre* in La Rochefoucauld', *French Review,* XLIII (1969-1970), 227-39.

22. Grandsaignes d'Hauterive, R. *Le Pessimisme de La Rochefoucauld.* Armand Colin, 1914, 222 pp.

23. Grubbs, Henry A. 'The originality of La Rochefoucauld's *Maxims*', *Revue d'Histoire Littéraire de la France,* XXXVI (1929), 18-59.

24. 'La Genèse des *Maximes* de La Rochefoucauld', *Revue d'Histoire Littéraire de la France,* XXXIX (1932), 481-99; XL (1933), 17-37.

25. Hippeau, Louis. *Essai sur la morale de la Rochefoucauld.* Nizet, 1967, 248 pp.

26. Ivanoff, N. *La Marquise de Sablé et son salon.* 1927, 246 pp.

27. James, E.D. 'Scepticism and Positive Values in La Rochefoucauld', *French Studies,* XXIII (1969), 349-61.

28. Kruse, Margot. *Die Maxime in der französischen Literatur. Studien zum Werk La Rochefoucaulds und seiner Nachfolger.* Hamburg, 1960, 224 pp.

29. Kuentz, Pierre. *Introduction aux 'Maximes'*, in *La Rochefoucauld, 'Maximes'*, Bordas, 1966.

30. Lafond, Jean. *La Rochefoucauld. Augustinisme et littérature.* Klincksieck, 1986 (troisième édition), 285 pp.

31. Lafond, Jean. 'L'Amour-propre de La Rochefoucauld' in *Ouverture et dialogue. Mélanges offerts à Wolfgang Leiner.* Tübingen, Narr, 1988, pp. 263-76.

32. Lafond, Jean. 'Augustinisme et épicurisme au XVIIe siècle', *XVIIe Siècle*, 135 (1982), 149-68.

33. Lafond, Jean. 'La Rochefoucauld, d'une culture à l'autre', *Cahiers de l'Association Internationale des Études Françaises*, XXX (1978), 155-69, 274-5.

34. Lafond, Jean. 'La Rochefoucauld et les enjeux de l'écriture', *Papers on French Seventeenth-Century Literature*, X, 19 (1983), 711-31.

35. Lafond, Jean. 'La Rochefoucauld moraliste'. *L'Information littéraire*, XXVIII (1976), 103-107.

36. Lafond, Jean, ed. *Les Formes brèves de la prose et le discours discontinu. Études réunies et présentées par Jean Lafond.* Vrin, 1984, 123 pp.

37. Lafond, Jean and Jean Mesnard, eds. *Images de La Rochefoucauld. Actes du Tricentenaire, 1680-1980.* Coordonnés par J. Lafond et J. Mesnard. Actes du Colloque d'Angoulême. Presses universitaires, 1984, 292 pp.

38. Lanson, Gustave. *L'Art de la prose.* Nizet, 1908 (pp. 133-9).

39. Leconte, Michelle. 'Recherches sur les dates de composition des *Réflexions diverses* de La Rochefoucauld'. *Revue des Sciences humaines*, XXX (1965), 177-89.

40. Levi, Anthony. *French Moralists. The Theory of the Passions, 1595-1649.* Oxford, Clarendon Press, 1964, 337 pp.

41. Levi, Anthony. 'Amour-propre. The Rise of an ethical concept', *The Month*, XCVI (1959), 283-94.

42. Lewis, Philip E. *La Rochefoucauld. The Art of Abstraction.* Ithaca and London, Cornell University Press, 1977, 191 pp.

43. Magne, Émile. *Le Vrai Visage de La Rochefoucauld.* Ollendorff, 1923, 198 pp.

44. Marvick, Louis W. 'The Function of Simile in the *Maximes* of La Rochefoucauld'. *Papers on French Seventeenth-Century Literature*, XVII, 34 (1991), 123-40.

45. Moore, W.G. *La Rochefoucauld. His Mind and Art.* Oxford, Clarendon Press, 1967, 134 pp.

46. Moriarty, Michael. *Taste and Ideology in Seventeenth-Century France.* Cambridge University Press, 1988, 241 pp.

47. Mourgues, Odette de. *Two French Moralists. La Rochefoucauld and La Bruyère.* Cambridge University Press, 1978, 181 pp.

48. Pagliaro, Harold E. 'Paradox in the Aphorisms of La Rochefoucauld and some Representative English Followers', *PMLA*, LXXIX (1964), 42-50.

49. Raymond, Marcel. 'Du Jansénisme à la morale de l'intérêt', *Mercure de France,* 330 (1957), 238-55.

50. Rosso, Corrado. *Procès à La Rochefoucauld et à la Maxime.* Pisa, Goliardica, 1986, 249 pp.

51. Rosso, Corrado. 'Démarches et structures de compensation dans les *Maximes*'. *C.A.I.E.F.,* XVIII (1966), 113-24; 262-70.

52. Sellier, Philippe. 'La Rochefoucauld, Pascal, Saint-Augustin'. *Revue d'Histoire littéraire de la France,* LXIX (1969), 551-75.

53. Starobinski, Jean. 'Complexité de La Rochefoucauld'. *Preuves,* 135 (1962), 33-40.

54. Starobinski, Jean. 'La Rochefoucauld ou l'oubli des secrets'. *Médecine de France,* 107 (1959), 33-40.

55. Starobinski, Jean. 'La Rochefoucauld et les morales substitutives'. *Nouvelle Revue Française,* XXVIII, 2 (1966), 16-34, 211-29.

56. Sutcliffe, F.E. 'The System of La Rochefoucauld'. *Bulletin of the John Rylands Library,* 49 (1966-1967), 233-45.

57. Thweatt, Vivien. *La Rochefoucauld and the Seventeenth-Century Concept of the Self.* Geneva, Droz, 1980, 279 pp.

58. Tocanne, Bernard. *L'Idée de nature en France dans la seconde moitié du dix-septième siècle.* Klincksieck, 1978, 498 pp.

59. Weber, Joseph G. 'The Personæ in the Style of La Rochefoucauld's *Maximes*'. *PMLA,* LXXXIX (1974), 250-55.

60. Westgate, D. 'The Concept of *Amour-propre* in the *Maximes* of La Rochefoucauld'. *Nottingham French Studies,* 7 (1968), 67-79.

61. Zeller, Mary F. *New Aspects of Style in the 'Maximes' of La Rochefoucauld.* Washington D.C., Catholic University of America Press, 1959, 174 pp.